a history of anthropological theory

for Dawn

a history of anthropological theory

Paul A. Erickson
with Liam D. Murphy

broadview press

NATIONAL LIBRARY OF CANADA CATALOGUING IN PUBLICATION DATA

Erickson, Paul A.
  A history of anthropological theory

ISBN 1-55111-198-5

1. Anthropology — Philosophy.   2. Anthropology — History.
I. Murphy, Liam Donat.   II. Title.

CN33.E74 1998   301'.01   C98-930325-X

BROADVIEW PRESS, LTD.
is an independent, international publishing house, incorporated in 1985.

North America	United Kingdom
Post Office Box 1243,	Thomas Lyster, Ltd.
Peterborough, Ontario,	Unit 9, Ormskirk Industrial Park
Canada K9J 7H5	Old Boundary Way, Burscough Rd.
Tel: (705) 743-8990	Ormskirk, Lancashire L39 2YW
Fax: (705) 743-8353	Tel: (01695) 575112
	Fax: (01695) 570120
3576 California Road,	books@tlyster.co.uk
Orchard Park, New York	
USA 14127	Australia
	St. Clair Press
customerservice@broadviewpress.com	P.O. Box 287, Rozelle, NSW 2039
www.broadviewpress.com	Tel: (612) 818-1942
	Fax: (612) 418-1923

Broadview Press gratefully acknowledges the financial support
of the Book Publishing Industry Development Program,
Ministry of Canadian Heritage, Government of Canada.

Text design and composition by George Kirkpatrick. Cover design by
Zack Taylor. Albrecht Dürer's *The Fall of Man* courtesy of Corbis, Inc.
Printed in Canada

contents

preface

In November, 1995, I organized a session of papers presented at the annual meeting of the American Anthropological Association exploring the theme "Teaching the History of Anthropological Theory: Strategies for Success." My own paper was a survey of courses in the history of anthropological theory taught at colleges and universities throughout Canada and the United States. The survey revealed that such courses are widespread in both graduate and undergraduate curricula. It also revealed that, owing to the diversified nature of anthropology, there is considerable variation in the scope of the courses and the way they are taught. Especially noteworthy are the great variation in texts and professors' serious dissatisfaction with their suitability. A recurring complaint of professors was, "We *need* a suitable textbook."

I have written *A History of Anthropological Theory* to help satisfy that need. The book is based on a senior-level undergraduate course that I have been teaching at Saint Mary's University for more than 20 years. Like the course, the book adopts the North American framework for anthropology as a general discipline with specialized subdisciplines of linguistic anthropology, archaeological anthropology, physical anthropology, and cultural anthropology. Most North American anthropology is cultural anthropology, so the book concentrates on this subdiscipline — but not exclusively. It includes important sections on archaeological and physical anthropology that can be read with profit by all anthropology students. Unlike many comparable texts, which begin in the eighteenth or nineteenth century, *A History of Anthropological Theory* begins in Antiquity, in the understanding that all subdisciplines of anthropology are deeply rooted in Western experience.

My course is a full-year course, equivalent to two semesters. The first half (or one semester) tells the history of anthropological theory prior to the twentieth century, the second half (another semester) during the twentieth century. Almost certainly the book cannot serve as the *only* text in courses of such scope. It can, however, serve as an introductory text, supplemented by lengthier, more detailed and special-interest texts, including primary-source "readers." Some professors may choose to use the book as a supplementary text in introductory general anthropology courses.

Experience leads me to believe that students in history of anthropological theory courses are usually prepared with background in one or more of the anthropology subdisciplines, but rarely in them all. For this reason, I have treated *A History of Anthropological Theory* as an introduction to the subject and attempted to write it in straightforward, non-polemical, and jargon-free prose. The book is also free of references to the voluminous history of anthropological theory scholarship. There are no scholarly footnotes or endnotes, only a list of follow-up recommended readings. A common lament of students in our courses — the majority of whom are enrolled not by choice, but because the course is a departmental major requirement — is the challenging vocabulary of theoretical "-isms" and "-ologies." To help ease their pain, I have attempted to define each challenging word or phrase the first time it is used meaningfully in the text, and at the end of the text I have appended a glossary of boldfaced terms. An added list of review questions should also help. Still, students should not be lulled into complacency. Learning (and teaching) the history of anthropological theory is usually difficult, although ultimately highly intellectually rewarding.

Like any course, my course has evolved through the incorporation of elements of the texts I have used on and off for years. These texts include Paul Bohannan and Mark Glazer's *High Points in Anthropology* (1989), Peter Bowler's *Evolution* (1989), Annemarie de Waal Malefijt's *Images of Man* (1974), Bruce Trigger's *A History of Archaeological*

Thought (1990), and Marvin Harris' *The Rise of Anthropological Theory* (1968) and *Cultural Materialism* (1979). Although *A History of Anthropological Theory* is not written from any of these authors' theoretical perspectives, its presentation and interpretation in places may be similar. In these places, I am indebted to the authors for inspiration and for an organization of material that, in the classroom, works. The emphasis on American, as opposed to British and French, anthropology is, however, my own. If theories or theoreticians appear to have been "left out," the reason is not disrespect, but a desire to keep the book brief.

I wrote *A History of Anthropological Theory* during the 1996-97 academic year while I was on sabbatical leave of absence from Saint Mary's University. I thank Saint Mary's for this valuable time away from teaching. I also thank anonymous reviewers and Michael Harrison, Barbara Conolly, and the staff of Broadview Press for evaluating the manuscript critically and suggesting ways to improve it. Outstanding recognition is owing to Liam Murphy of Yale University, who critiqued the entire manuscript and wrote the sections on "The Legacy of Max Weber," "Symbolic and Interpretive Anthropology," "Political Economy," and "Postmodernism." Neither he nor anyone else, however, should be held accountable for errors encountered in the book.

As always, my wife Dawn Erickson provided constant encouragement and support (and some necessary prodding), for which I shall be forever grateful.

Paul A. Erickson
Halifax, Nova Scotia

The course on which *A History of Anthropological Theory* is based is one I took while an undergraduate at Saint Mary's University. It is hardly an exaggeration to say that what I learned that year had a deep and enduring influence on me, and is at least part of the reason why I decided to become a professional anthropologist. So when Paul

Erickson asked me to critically review the manuscript of his new book, based on that same course, I was extremely flattered. After all, it is not everyday that former students are given the opportunity to throw in their "two cents" in this way. When subsequently asked to contribute several sections, I was only too happy to oblige. My first debt of thanks, therefore, must be to Paul for all the advice and encouragement he has given me, both as a teacher and a friend, over the years. They have been invaluable. I would also like to thank Dawn Erickson for her friendship, which I also value greatly. And as always, my parents, Arthur and Patricia Murphy, have been a constant source of love and support without whom my career in anthropology would probably not even exist.

Liam D. Murphy
Belfast, Northern Ireland

The History of Anthropological Theory Before 1900

The Enlightenment	1800	1900
The Scientific Revolution	1700	Evolutionism vs. Diffusionism
	1600	
		1890
Voyages of Geographical Discovery	1500	
The Renaissance	1400	1880
	1300	
	1200	
		1870
	1100	
		Classical Cultural Evolutionism
	1000	
		1860 Darwinism
	900	
		Archaeology Comes of Age
	800	
		1850 Marxism
The Middle Ages	700	
	600	
		1840
	500	
	400	
		1830
	300	
	200	
		1820 The Rise of Positivism
	100	
	0	
		1810
	100	
	200	
		1800
Anthropology in Antiquity		
	300	

The History of Anthropological Theory After 1900

2000

1990   **Postmodernism**

1980   **Political Economy**

Biologized Anthropology

Symbolic and Interpretive Anthropology

1970   **The Legacy of Max Weber**

Cultural Materialism

French Structural Anthropology   **1960**   **Cultural Neo-Evolutionism**

Cognitive Anthropology

1950   **Development of Psychological Anthropology**

British Social Anthropology

1940   **The Influence of Sigmund Freud**

Margaret Mead and Ruth Benedict

1930

Robert Lowie and Alfred Louis Koeber

1920

The Influence of Émile Durkheim

1910   **Franz Boas**

1900

chapter one: the early history of anthropological theory

Introduction to Anthropology

Anthropology is a fascinating field of study of all peoples past and present. In North America, the field is traditionally divided into four subfields. The first subfield, physical, or biological, anthropology is concerned with the evolutionary origins and diversity of the species *Homo sapiens*. Physical anthropologists include paleoanthropologists, who study human fossils; primatologists, who study our monkey, ape and related evolutionary "cousins"; and human geneticists. The second subfield, archaeological anthropology, is the study of artifacts, or the material remains of past human activity. Prehistoric archaeologists specialize in studying the artifacts of peoples without written records, while historical archaeologists specialize in studying the artifacts of peoples with written records. Archaeologists cooperate with a wide range of other specialists, including geologists, biologists, and historians. The third subfield, linguistic anthropology, is concerned with the nature of language, and with the nature, history, and social function of the multitude of particular languages spoken and written around the world. The fourth subfield, cultural, or sociocultural, anthropology is the study of human lifeways and thoughts, often summed up as "culture." Cultural anthropologists, the most numerous of anthropologists, specialize in studying one or more cultural groups and domains, such as Inuit art, Hopi religion, and Australian aboriginal kinship. Taken together, these four subfields give anthropology a uniquely "holistic," or broad-based and overarching, world view. Anthropologists are quick to assert that any statement about "human nature" must pertain to the biological and cultural nature of *everybody*.

A conspicuous trend in late twentieth-century anthropology, at least in North America, has been the diversification of the traditional subfields into an increasing number of special interest groups. Arguably, this trend began with the addition of a "fifth" subfield, applied anthropology, designed to accommodate the interests of anthropologists finding employment outside universities and museums. The trend has continued to the point where, in the late 1990s, the American Anthropological Association, the largest association of professional anthropologists in the world, was divided into some 30 special-interest sections. These sections have interests as diverse as those represented, for example, by the Association for Feminist Anthropology, Council on Nutritional Anthropology, Society for Urban Anthropology, Society for the Anthropology of Europe and Society for the Anthropology of Consciousness. Under circumstances of such diversity, anthropology, prone to introspection anyway, was bound to intensify its efforts to understand just what it stands for theoretically.

"Theory" in anthropology stands for different things in different anthropological circles. By invoking broad, often unstated, definitions such as "general orientation," "guiding principle," and "intellectual framework," anthropologists have been able to discuss theory without always having to articulate just what it means to themselves or to others. This is particularly true in the "history of anthropological theory," an established topic of anthropological discussion in which "original," "important," and "influential" theories and theorists are identified relatively easily in hindsight. Such theories and theorists become "canonized" simply by being referred to as original, important, and influential by a sufficient number of anthropologists over a sufficient period of time. They then form lineages of theoretical ancestors, in which descendants position themselves to gain theoretical identity.

In most North American colleges and universities, undergraduate anthropology majors and graduate students complete a course or course unit in the history of anthropological theory. The main manifest, or explicit, function of this experience is to enhance the theoretical sophistication of students and to introduce them to theories and theorists with whom they might not otherwise become acquainted. The latent, or implicit, function of the experience is to serve as a rite of passage, in which new generations of anthropologists "join the club" by recapitulating its intellectual history. Approached as a "dialogue with the ancestors," rather than "one dead guy a week,"[1] the history of anthropological theory can be exciting, thought-provoking, and moving. It can also be humbling and nurture respect, as "younger" anthropologists realize that they are heirs to an anthropological legacy that is time-honoured and, in the main, noble.

Any history of anthropological theory is written by a particular historian at a particular time and in a particular place. A respectable historian aims to be truthful but cannot, of course, expect to achieve "*the* truth, the whole truth, and nothing but the truth." This is because the historian must select elements from the past and put them together in a way that makes sense in the present, which is always changing. The inevitable result is that the historian's analytical categories may seem "imposed" on the past, rendering, for example, certain early figures and ideas "unfairly" proto-anthropological. By selecting certain past figures and their ideas, and by interpreting them in light of subsequent events to which we know they (often unwittingly) contributed, the historian can help us understand where anthropology came from and, therefore, what it really is.

In the analytical perspective adopted in this book, theoretically anthropology can be considered to be a branch of science, humanism or religion. The differences among science, humanism, and religion have to do with how these three systems of thought treat the relationship among nature, people, and God. In science, people and God are treated as secondary to nature, which is paramount in the sense that nature encompasses people and God. In the science of biology, for example, people are considered to be composed of pre-existing natural elements like carbon and water, while in the science of psychiatry, or at least some versions of it, God is considered to be created by a pre-existing human brain. In humanism, God and nature are treated as secondary to people, who are paramount in the sense that people encompass God and nature. Examples of humanism can be found in literature and philosophy, where "Man is the measure of all things" and "human nature," especially creatively expressed, is the central fact of existence. Finally, in religion, nature and people are treated as secondary to God, who is paramount in the sense that God encompasses nature and people. A familiar example of religion is the Judeo-Christian belief, expressed in the Bible, that God created "heaven and earth" and, within a few days, Adam and Eve. Throughout its history, anthropology has been, in terms of these definitions, variously scientific, humanistic, and religious.

Beneath these theoretical complexities, anthropology can be seen to be searching for answers to fundamental questions asked by people everywhere, such as "Where did we come from?," "Why do we differ?," and "How does the world work?" Confronting an avalanche of technical information in books, articles, and reports, anthropologists sometimes forget that these questions are universal and, therefore, that all peoples have their own versions of anthropology. The version relevant to most readers of this book is the one that derives from Western civilization.

Anthropology in Antiquity

In the West, beginning in Antiquity a few centuries before the birth of Christ, Greco-Roman civilization produced several Classical intellectual traditions. Today, following the account of Annemarie de Waal Malefijt in *Images of Man*, some of these traditions seem scientific, or at least quasi-scientific, while others, such as the epic poetry of Homer (*circa* 8th century B.C.) and Vergil (70-19 B.C.), appear more humanistic or religious. The roots of what most of us today would call anthropology can be found in the efforts at early Classical science.

The first group of Classical thinkers with a semblance of science were those philosophers whose thought predates that of Socrates, teacher of Plato. The pre-Socratics were really cosmologists, who speculated on the origin and nature of the cosmos, or embodied world. Some of these speculations were materialistic, meaning that they invoked natural rather than supernatural causes. One such pre-Socratic was the Greek philosopher Thales (*c*.640–*c*.546), who speculated that everything in the world came from water. Another was Anaximander (*c*.622–*c*.547), a pupil of Thales, who said that the original substance of the cosmos was not a known element, but "something boundless" and undifferentiated. A third pre-Socratic was Empedocles (*c*.490–*c*.430), sometimes called an ancient precursor of Darwin. Empedocles believed that the cosmos evolved as different constituent elements encountered one another and formed larger bodies that survived if they were useful, a process vaguely resembling natural selection. Finally, an extreme version of pre-Socratic materialism is represented by Democritus (*c*.460–*c*.370), who proposed that human bodies, minds, and behaviour derived from changes in the shape, size, and velocity of constantly-moving universal particles, or "atoms." Like other pre-Socratics, Democritus opposed the idea of a human "Golden Age," from which people had allegedly deteriorated. Instead, he saw progress and betterment in the working of natural forces.

Pre-Socratic science was not modern, of course, but it *was* different from ancient humanism and from the religion in ancient Greek myths like that of Prometheus, a primordial deity said to have made people out of clay and stolen fire for them from Mount Olympus. Pre-Socratic philosophers saw people created by nature, not gods.

Another ancient Greek tradition more scientific than religious was the tradition of travel writing, best represented by Herodotus (*c*.484–*c*.425), the "Father of History." In his travels beyond the limited world of ancient Greece, Herodotus observed diversity in race, language, and culture. He explained this diversity in a relatively objective, or non-ethnocentric, way, by correlating it with geography, climate, and other features of the natural world. Herodotus was also humanistic, because he stressed how human differences were caused by human, not divine, acts. This combination of science and humanism, as opposed to religion, makes his writing a kind of ancient precursor of ethnography.

In the fifth century B.C., there was a major change in Greek life when democracy in the city-state of Athens superseded the older political system based on kinship. This fundamental shift in politics was accompanied by a shift in thought, leading to new philosophical schools. One new school was Sophistry, which taught that practical skills and social effectiveness were goals more important than the search for objective knowledge or absolute truth. The Sophist Protagoras (c.481-c.411), to whom some attribute the phrase "Man is the measure of all things," believed that human behaviour is not influenced by gods but by life circumstances. Behaviour, then, is really cultural convention, and should be seen as such — a doctrine not cultural relativism   unlike the twentieth-century doctrine of cultural relativism. Protagoras also explained how various cultural conventions may have come about through an evolutionary-like process. For some Sophists, relativism led to Nihilism, the doctrine that nothing exists or is knowable. They became Nihilists because they felt that virtues were not absolute and that knowledge was merely what was said to be true by people in power — an idea that adumbrates a key part of the nineteenth century doctrine of Marxism. Even in the fifth century B.C., broad anthropological ideas had begun to take root.

Some important Athenian philosophers were opposed to Sophistry. Socrates (c.469-399) taught that there *were* universal values, even though they were difficult to perceive and express. People had to train their minds for these tasks. Education was important, according to Socrates, because it enabled people to see through their cultural conventions, not merely manipulate them, as the Sophists advocated. Plato (c.427-347), the famous student of Socrates, agreed with his teacher that there were universal values. These values existed because they were innate in the human mind. According to Plato, people recognize objects because, before they perceive them, they have the *idea* of them. His *Republic* was a dialogue about an ideal society constructed on the basis of people's perceptions of flaws in real societies. Plato reconstructed the development of society through time in order to show what had changed and what had remained the same. What had remained the same were transcendental "essences" of things.

The philosopher Aristotle (384-322), Plato's student, agreed with Plato that society had developed over time, but he was much more empirical, examining the development of society in its own right rather than trying to pierce through it to a universal, transcendental realm. Aristotle was curious about the relationships among natural and social objects, which he assumed existed and were knowable. Contrasted with Plato, whose idea of transcendental essences became incorporated into religion, the legacy of Aristotle included science, inherited through Alexander the Great (356-323), whom Aristotle tutored. When Alexander the Great conquered the Greek city states and the Persian Empire from India to Asia Minor and Egypt, founding the Egyptian city of Alexandria in 332 B.C., the scientific teachings of Aristotle spread.

Socrates, Plato, and Aristotle lived in the "Golden Age of Greece." After Alexander the Great died, the unity of Greek life and thought declined, and competing schools of thought emerged. Epicurus (c.342-270) pursued Empedocles' belief that people comprised atoms, which were dissolved at death and reabsorbed into nature. Epicurus was an extreme utilitarian in that he considered society to be a mechanical extension of humanity and therefore subservient to humanity. Later, the Roman poet Lucretius (c.96-c.55) expressed these views more forcefully in his materialistic poem *On The Nature of Things*.

Meanwhile, the Stoics, like the Epicureans, wanted a correct and happy life, but, unlike the Epicureans, believed that nature and society were highly orderly. According to the Stoic philosopher Zeno (c.336-c.264), this order was not created by people or gods, but was a natural cosmic order, sometimes called Logos. This concept was later co-opted by early Christian theologians seeking to defend their beliefs against various schools of Greek philosophy. Belief in a universal social order made it possible to compare and contrast particular social orders, a fundamental task of what today we call social science. Furthermore, according to the Stoics, matter, not mind, is real; matter can be perceived; and learning is the perception of matter. Therefore, contrary to Plato, the Stoics believed in what was later *tabula rasa* called **tabula rasa**, or "blank slate," meaning a mind that acquires knowledge through experience rather than recognizes knowledge that is innate.

Stoicism was the philosophical bridge between the Greeks and the Romans, forming the philosophical basis for Rome's great advances in political organization and theory. In Rome, the idea of a natural order was developed into the concept of cosmopolis, or world citizenry, by statesman and orator Marcus Tullius Cicero (106-43). At the same time, other Roman writers like Seneca (4 B.C.- 65 A.D.) and Marcus Aurelius (121-180 A.D.) used the concept to explore humanistic and religious themes, paving the way for its eventual attachment to Christianity. In both realms, secular and religious, Stoicism encouraged people to make their particular thoughts and actions accord with something universal, while telling them that, as rational beings, they were capable of this achievement. Such a philosophy is one of the great legacies of Antiquity.

Toward the end of the Roman Empire, social conditions deteriorated, and several religions competed for appeal to the socially oppressed, all building on the Stoic idea of an overarching supernatural order in the universe. At first, these religions, or sects, were outlawed, because they preached obedience to divine rather than civil law. Prominent among them were Mithraism, Orphism, the cults of Cybele, Isis, and Osiris — and Christianity. Outpacing the competition, Christianity gained converts and (ironically for a religion of the oppressed) became the state religion of Rome under Emperor Constantine I (Constantine "The Great") (*c*.288-337). This action led in the fourth century A. D. to the Patristic period of Church history, during which time Church doctrine was established by Church "Fathers."

For anthropology, the most consequential Church Father was the Bishop of Hippo in northern Africa, Saint Augustine (354-430), author of *The City of God* and *Confessions*. The Augustinian version of Christianity was the version that prevailed when the Roman Empire declined and Europe entered the Middle Ages.

Major tenets of Augustinian Christianity were not conducive to science, especially social, or human, science. According to Augustine, God was perfect and human nature was sinful. The cosmos and humanity were not in harmony. The cosmos had been created by an omnipotent, or all-powerful, God, who was inscrutable, or unknowable. Therefore, it was pointless for people to study God or nature. Human behaviour was to be judged not by people or nature, but by God. Finally, everything people could know about themselves, nature, and God was revealed in Scripture. These tenets, designed to account for the mystery of God, had the effect of smothering human curiosity and the sense that nature, too, is mysterious. Without mysteries and the curiosity to solve them, why bother to develop science?

On the positive side for science, and later for anthropology, Augustinian Christianity did stress the importance of history, because it was from history, as revealed in Scripture, that Christians could learn at least something about God. Furthermore, Augustinian history was lineal, not cyclical, and it was a universal history, not just the history of "nations." These tenets laid the broad foundation for the temporal and spatial, or cross-cultural, perspectives of anthropology.

The legacy of Antiquity to anthropology, then, was the establishment of the humanistic, religious, and scientific intellectual outlooks. In various guises, and in different times and places, these outlooks, especially the scientific outlook, have persevered in anthropology ever since.

The Middle Ages

Following Augustine's death, the Western Roman Empire declined and was occupied by non-Christian "barbarians" and "pagans." The Christian tradition continued to flourish, however, in the Eastern Roman, or Byzantine, Empire, with its capital at Constantinople, founded by Constantine I in 330 A.D. There, and in pockets elsewhere, monastic Christian historians and encyclopedists like Isidore of Seville (c. 560-636) denounced barbarians and pagans while they kept the teachings of Augustine alive.

Meanwhile, the pre-Christian intellectual traditions of Antiquity were kept alive by Middle Eastern Semitic peoples who, following the birth of the prophet Mohammed *circa* 570 A.D., spread the Islamic religion out of Arabia, across northern Africa, and all the way to Spain. Contrasted with early Christians, who embraced the transcendental and otherworldly qualities of Platonism, Arab intellectuals like Ibn Khaldûn (1332-1406) had great respect for Aristotelian logic and science. More forcefully than Plato, Aristotle counteracted the scientifically negative attitude of Augustine that people were incapable of knowing nature and that nature, except through God, was incapable of being known. When Islam and Augustinian Christianity interacted, Christian theology changed.

The critical interaction between Islam and Christianity occurred in the eighth century when Islamic Moors invaded Christian Spain. Afterward, Christian theology became increasingly "rational," meaning that human reason was brought to bear on theological issues. This trend culminated in the theology of Thomas Aquinas (c. 1225-1274), author of *Summa Theologica* (1267-1273), one of the great treatises of the Roman Catholic Church. Thomistic Christianity (as the theology of Thomas Aquinas is called) differed radically from Augustinian Christianity. Unlike Augustine, Aquinas reasoned that people could, and should, know God through knowing nature. The true essence of humanity was not of sin only, but also of the kernel of the divinity created within each human being. Human reason was a gift of God, and people were morally responsible to use this gift to glorify God by learning about God's creation, the natural world. Human reason could even be used to prove the existence of God. In Thomistic Christianity, God, people, and nature were harmonized into a self-contained intellectual system without internal contradictions. Nothing people discovered about nature through the exercise of their God-given reason could cast doubt on the credibility and authority of God or on his representative Church on Earth — or so it was thought.

In order to keep Thomistic Christianity intact, it was necessary to ensure that science remained consistent with the Word of God. This was the job of numerous scholarly "commentators," who interpreted the writings of Aristotle and Church Fathers opportunistically. Scholasticism, as the doctrine supporting this activity came to be called, predominated in the Middle Ages. It has been caricatured as "seeing how many angels can be fitted onto the head of a pin." Inevitably, cracks in the whole system surfaced, and when it became impossible, or simply too difficult, to reconcile science and religion, scholars began to choose one over the other. Once this happened, the door was open for anthropology to develop, by contemporary standards, along scientific lines.

The Renaissance

The intellectual unity achieved by Thomistic Christianity was a kind of medieval synthesis. The synthesis unified the three elements whose varied relationships define science, humanism, and religion: i.e., nature, people, and God. Intellectually precarious from the start, it did not last long. Three complex events produced knowledge that, outside Thomistic circles, made the synthesis unravel. These events were the Renaissance, voyages of geographical discovery, and the Scientific Revolution, each of which shaped modern anthropology in critically important ways.

The Renaissance was a revival of interest in ancient learning whose beginning marks the transition from the medieval to the modern world. The key developments took place from the fourteenth through the sixteenth centuries in the nuclear city-states of Western Europe, especially northern Italy. There, wealthy mercantilists and other members of the prospering middle class began to spend their money as "patrons" of artists and scientists who were unwilling to accept pronouncements of the Church. The archetypical

"Renaissance Man" was the Italian painter, sculptor, architect, musician, engineer, and mathematician Leonardo da Vinci (1452-1519). Like other creative geniuses of the Renaissance, da Vinci was enamoured of the ancient world, because the ancient world represented a pre-Christian source of knowledge and values. Curiosity about the ancient world also produced classical archaeology, which developed during the Renaissance as an effort to use classical artifacts to supplement what was written in classical texts. In Italy, the rediscovery of Roman Antiquity was especially exhilarating, because Rome was part of Italy's own "glorious past." Renaissance thinkers came to realize that the Ancients possessed a fuller and more satisfying grasp of human nature than did the austere Christians of the Middle Ages.

Renaissance interest in the ancient world produced a new sense of time, which no longer seemed static, but capable of producing change — change as dramatic as that represented by the difference between the ancient and medieval worlds. This realization led to a systematic contrast of ancient and medieval ways of life and, in turn, to a questioning of the authority of the medieval Catholic Church based on a preference for secular alternatives from the past. In the history of religion, this trend led to the Protestant reform movements of the sixteenth century. In the histories of humanism and science, it continued to broaden the secularization of thinking, paving the way for the emergence of the modern tradition of scholarly social criticism and analysis.

Three influential social critics and analysts inspired by the Renaissance outlook were Desiderius Erasmus (c.1466-1536), Thomas More (1478-1535), and Niccolò Machiavelli (1469-1527). In *The Praise of Folly* (1509), Dutchman Erasmus opposed the idea of original sin, arguing that Greek virtues incorporated into early Christianity were superior to virtues espoused by later Christianity, which had grown excessively formal, bureaucratic, and corrupt. His highly irreverent book poked fun at the perceived stupidity, greed, and hypocrisy of priests and monks. In *Utopia* (1516), Englishman More contrasted the evils of contemporary society with the virtues of a society constructed on secular principles and based on ethnographic accounts of

original sin

Adam and Eve.

This Renaissance engraving depicts Adam and Eve being expelled from the Garden of Eden, an act of profound consequence in the Judeo-Christian account of human creation. [Albrecht Dürer (1471-1528), Nuremburg, Germany, engraving. Centennial gift of Landon T. Clay. Courtesy, Museum of Fine Arts, Boston.]

"simpler" peoples, whose lives were happier because they lacked private property, money, and crime. In *The Prince* (1513), Italian Machiavelli described the qualities of an effective political ruler, who must be strong, intelligent, and wise enough to understand the good and bad parts of human nature. All three of these influential Renaissance thinkers show that by the early sixteenth century there

had emerged a strong tradition of secular social analysis that later, in
cross-cultural analysis anthropology, would become **cross-cultural analysis**. The main
Renaissance legacy to anthropology was this secular, critical
approach.

Voyages of Geographical Discovery

During the late Roman Imperial period, Saint Augustine pro-
antipodes nounced, "No antipodes exist." **Antipodes** were places on opposite
sides of the world, including the people who live there. In making this
pronouncement, Augustine was expressing the view, widely held at
the time, that most parts of the world had already been discovered,
that nothing dramatically different remained to be found. Augustine
was mistaken. Between Roman and early modern times, enough geographical exploration had taken place to bring Europeans into contact with peoples different enough from themselves to be questioned
as truly human.

European exploration began in earnest with the eleventh-century
Christian crusades to Africa and parts of the Middle East. Exploration
expanded in the thirteenth century when the Mongols conquered
much of the Holy Roman Empire in central and eastern Europe. One
of the most famous European explorers was Venetian Marco Polo
(c.1254-c.1324), who spent 17 years in China at the court of the
Mongol ruler Kublai Khan. Intense competition for profitable trade
routes to Asia spurred further exploration by Portugal and Spain. By
1499, Vasco da Gama (c.1469-1524) found his way around Africa to
India, while a few years earlier, in 1492, seeking the same destination,
Christopher Columbus (c.1446-1506) discovered the "New World."
When Vasco Núñez de Balboa (c.1475-1517) sailed around South
America and discovered the Pacific Ocean in 1513, it became clear
that the New World was in fact new (to Europeans). The first round
of European exploration was concluded by Ferdinand Magellan
(c.1480-1521), who circumnavigated the globe.

No other event in history was as significant for anthropology as the
voyages of geographical discovery. The voyages put Europeans in

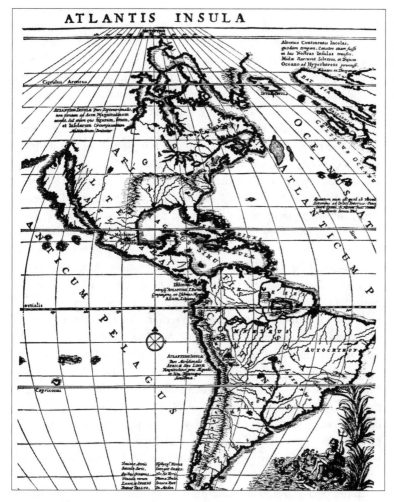

The New World.

This seventeenth-century map depicts the New World as the "Island of Atlantis."

contact with the kinds of people anthropologists now study. They also launched the era of global domination of aboriginal societies by Europeans, and the associated eras of colonialism, imperialism, and slavery, with which anthropology has, justly or unjustly, been associated ever since.

European initial opinions of non-European aborigines presented a major challenge to the medieval synthesis of God, people, and nature.

To Europeans, the aborigines, especially the "Indian" aborigines of the New World, appeared extraordinarily different, far too primitive and savage to belong to a single family of God's creation. Thomas Aquinas, who knew something about human diversity, had pronounced that aboriginal natives were imperfect humans and therefore

natural slaves **natural slaves** to Europeans. At the time, this pronouncement seemed plausible, but problems with it quickly arose. Imperfect natural slaves lacked the mental and moral capacity for free agency, or the ability to make a conscious choice. Without free agency, natives could not make a valid conversion to Christianity as a means of achieving salvation. Therefore, they were denied the kingdom of God, rendering the efforts of missionaries futile.

Christian theology had to change, and it did. Influential Spanish theologians Bartolomé de Las Casas (1474-1566) and José de Acosta

natural children (c.1539-1600) redefined natural slaves as **natural children**, allowing benevolence to "save" them and make them civilized Christians. An important consequence of this redefinition, in theological terms, was to bring the human family closer together. But if all the peoples of the world were to belong to the same family, should not they be historically connected? The Protestant Reformation had made the Bible the sole authority on history for most of Christian Europe. A few Biblical passages did imply historical connections, for example through Adam and Eve, the sons of Noah, and tribes dispersed after destruction of the Tower of Babel. By and large, however, Biblical support for the idea that *all* the peoples of the world were God's children was scant and, in some circles, insufficient. Additional support was needed.

In the period from the sixteenth through the eighteenth centuries, several ingenious schemes were designed to show that Europeans were historically connected to non-Europeans, especially to American Indians, with whom, following the colonization of America, Europeans were being forced to interact. According to one scheme, Indians were descendants of survivors of the sunken continent of Atlantis, a relationship purportedly demonstrated by cultural similarities between Europeans and the Incas and Aztecs. Another

yeqtla ti tetzavitl
yn mal ques.

The Old World Meets the New.
Early sixteenth-century Spanish soldiers besiege the Aztec capital of Tenochtitlán.

scheme made Indians one of the ten Lost Tribes of Israel, while yet another, foreshadowing the modern scientific view, had them immigrating to America from northern Asia across the Bering Strait. Gradually, these schemes, inspired by the desire to reconcile natural observations with Christian theology, became more "scientific." In anthropology, they led to **monogenesis**, the doctrine that human races constitute a single biological species, with a common origin and physical differences produced by natural agents over time. In the nineteenth century, monogenesis faced stiff competition from **polygenesis**, the doctrine that human races constitute separate species, with separate origins and physical differences that are unalterable and racially innate. Debate between monogenesists and polygenesists reached its peak in the heyday of classical nineteenth-century anthropology.

monogenesis

polygenesis

The Scientific Revolution

A paramount reason for the change of medieval into modern times was the Scientific Revolution, meaning the invention of modern science as a method of intellectual investigation and the growth of specialized sciences and their accumulated bodies of knowledge about the natural world. Because all anthropologists entertain some vision of the "correct" scientific method, modern anthropology is rooted in these momentous events.

There are two parts to the Scientific Revolution: the growth of scientific epistemologies and the accumulation of scientific knowledge.

epistemology   **Epistemology** is the branch of philosophy that explores the nature of knowledge. In the post-medieval era, when the intellectual authority of the Church was eroding, new epistemologies for science were required. Two major epistemologies emerged, both of which are employed by the practising scientist today. One epistemology is

deduction   **deduction**, the use of logic to reason from general to particular statements or, defined more broadly, the process of drawing a conclusion from something known or assumed. Deduction is used in all sciences, especially the formal sciences of mathematics. The most famous intellectual architect of deduction was French mathematician René Descartes (1596-1650), who reasoned, "I exist, therefore God exists, therefore the real world exists." The Cartesian (the adjectival form of Descartes) version of deduction laid the foundation for the scientific

French rationalism   tradition of **French rationalism**. A central tenet of Cartesian thought, and one that was to become pivotal in postmodern theory (discussed in a later chapter) is that it assumes the essential duality of the world divided into objects and subjects, the rational and the irrational, the cultural and the natural.

induction   The second epistemology is **induction**, the process of discovering general explanations for particular facts by weighing the observational evidence for propositions that make assertions about those facts. The most famous intellectual architects of induction were English philosophers Francis Bacon (1561-1626) and John Locke (1632-

1704), whose ideas formed an important part of the eighteenth-century Enlightenment. Baconian and Lockean versions of induction laid the foundation for the scientific tradition of **British empiricism**. Both French rationalism and British empiricism have had followers in anthropology.

British empiricism

From the thirteenth through the seventeenth centuries, increasingly powerful applications of scientific epistemologies supplanted medieval ways of thinking to produce a series of scientific discoveries culminating in the revolutionary scientific synthesis of Sir Isaac Newton. The story of this revolution begins with **mechanics**, the science of motion, and with **cosmology**, a branch of philosophy concerned with the origin and structure of the universe.

mechanics
cosmology

Medieval mechanics and cosmology derived from a combination of Christian theology and Aristotelian science. In the medieval world view, the Earth was the centre of the universe, and all bodies moved to the centre of the Earth in a form of motion that was considered natural. All other motion was considered unnatural, and needed a mover to be explained. In unnatural motion, if a body ceased being moved, it would stop, or come to rest. The speed of a moving body depended on the force of the mover, with a constant force producing a constant speed. When a moving body met resistance, its speed would decrease. If the resistance decreased, its velocity would increase proportionately so that, in a vacuum, where there is no resistance at all, its speed should be instantaneous. To medieval scientists, the concept of instantaneous speed seemed absurd. Therefore, there *was* no vacuum. Besides, God would not like a vacuum anyway!

In this system, naturally falling bodies should not accelerate, or pick up speed. But they did. The solution to this problem, devised by medieval commentators, was to posit that air rushed in behind falling bodies, forcing them downward. As the height of the air beneath falling bodies decreased, they met less resistance and accelerated. This solution worked well for a while, then became unconvincing. There was the added problem of projectiles, or bodies impelled forward through the air. Why did projectiles slow down? According to a theory developed in the 1300s, projectiles were given the property of impetus, which spent itself in flight. By the same token, naturally falling bodies *acquired* impetus, which made them accelerate. The theory of impetus, a classic *ad hoc* explanation, was a bridge between medieval theories and the modern theory of inertia.

Medieval mechanics was an integral part of medieval cosmology. In medieval cosmology, the earthly domain was cut off from the celestial, or spiritual, domain by the four elements of earth, water, air, and fire, which covered the Earth in layered orbs, or spheres. The celestial orbs comprised a fifth element, something unchanging and eternal. There were ten celestial orbs, the outer one the empyrean heaven. Aristotle had proclaimed these orbs real, although frictionless. Ptolemy (127-151), the great Greek astronomer at Alexandria, was forced to add almost 80 additional orbs, with epicycles, smaller circles moving around the circumference of larger circles, to account for "irregularities" in planetary motion. This solution created a major new problem: the orbs, supposedly real, intersected.

In 1543, Polish astronomer Nicholaus Copernicus (1473-1543) helped launch the Scientific Revolution by announcing that the Earth moved around the Sun, not the other way around, and that the Earth revolved on its own axis. Copernicus intended his action, which reduced the number of required orbs to 34, to be conservative, bolstering the Ptolemaic system by salvaging elements of it that still worked. But the implications were ominous. If the Earth was not the centre of the universe, how could it be special? How could God have created it for the glorification of people? Were there other worlds? Moreover, this solution created new technical problems and was beset by new nonconforming observations. If the Earth was rotating on its axis, why did falling bodies not land *behind* where they were dropped? Also, in the late 1500s, new stars and comets appeared, and their paths of movement, especially those of the comets, cut through the celestial orbs. To solve this problem, Danish astronomer Tycho Brahe (1546-1601) took the next bold step by announcing that the orbs did not exist. Then, in the early 1600s, German astronomer Johann Kepler (1571-1630), freed from the constraints of orbs, described planetary orbits as ellipses rather than perfect circles. Kepler's laws of planetary motion had planets moving around the Sun and sweeping equal areas in equal time, implying that planets closer to the Sun moved faster.

Meanwhile, Italian physicist and astronomer Galileo Galilei (1564-1642) used the telescope to observe sun spots and other "blemishes" on heavenly bodies. Reflecting on the revolutionary views of his predecessors, Galileo, in *Dialogue Concerning the Two Chief Systems of the World* (1632), systematically contrasted the Ptolemaic and Copernican world views. In the process, he solved the problem of falling bodies not landing behind where they were dropped by reasoning that everything on the Earth rotates with it; in other words, "behind" does not really exist. Still, two huge interrelated problems remained: what *caused* motion on Earth, now that the Earth was no longer the centre of the universe, and what *caused* celestial bodies to move, now that there were no orbs?

These remaining problems were solved by British scientist Isaac Newton (1642-1727), who, in *Principles of Mathematics* (1687), showed that one law, the law of universal gravitation, accounted for the motion of bodies both on Earth and in the celestial realm. Newton showed that all bodies move by being attracted to one another with a force proportional to the square of the distance between them. Bodies on Earth move because they are attracted to the Earth (and the Earth to them), and celestial bodies move because they are attracted to one another in patterns consistent with Kepler's laws of planetary motion. Contrasted with the medieval system, Newton's system maintains that inertia keeps bodies moving unless they are affected by new forces, rendering it unnecessary to keep bodies moving by constantly applying the same force. Moreover, a constant force produces constant acceleration, not speed. The Newtonian cosmos is one law-bound system of matter in motion, with the Earth and its inhabitants careening through empty space in a way that scientists do not have to invoke God to explain. For his intellectual achievements, Isaac Newton was knighted and buried in Westminster Abbey. Many years later, Charles Darwin was buried nearby — "the Newton of biology."

The significance of the Scientific Revolution for anthropology is twofold. First, the world conceived by Newton is the world most

law of universal gravitation

modern anthropologists accept. Second, Newton's accomplishments in natural science inspired similar efforts in the social sphere. The result was that in the century following Newton, the eighteenth-century Enlightenment, the seeds of social science were planted, took root, and flourished.

The Enlightenment

Enlightenment The **Enlightenment** is the name given to the intellectual history of Europe in the eighteenth century, from the time of Newton's *Principles of Mathematics* to the time of the French Revolution, beginning in 1789. During this period, following fast on the Scientific Revolution, intellectual attitudes coalesced to produce key concepts of social science. In anthropology, the most important of these concepts was culture.

In a way, the Enlightenment was a continuation of the Scientific Revolution, because Enlightenment intellectuals were so enamoured of the philosophy of Newton that they extended it from the natural mechanical philosophy into the social realm. Newton's philosophy was called the **mechanical philosophy**, referring to his image of the universe as a complex machine with fine-tuned, interacting parts. The machine was always moving, and the job of the scientist was to learn just how. His phi-deistic losophy was also called **deistic**, because Newton believed that God had theistic *created* the universe while, unlike a **theistic** philosopher, he did not invoke God to account for its day-to-day machinations. Metaphorically, the Newtonian universe was a clock, God the clockmaker.

Another major figure in the Enlightenment was British philosopher John Locke (1632-1704), who in *An Essay Concerning Human Understanding* (1690) expanded the scientific epistemology of British empiricism. For anthropology, the most important part of Locke's epistemology was his idea, resurrected from the ancient Stoics, that the mind of each newborn person is a *tabula rasa*, or "blank slate," "written on" by life. What made this philosophy so important is that it was a philosophy of experience, in which human thoughts and behaviour were understood to be acquired rather than inherited or in some other way innate. Such an understanding was indispensable for the emergence of the concept of culture, which can be defined here as the accumulated way of living created and acquired by people and transmitted from one generation to another extrasomatically, other than through genes. Culture is the central concept of American anthropology. Its emergence during the Enlightenment is the reason why American anthropologist Marvin Harris argues in *The Rise of Anthropological Theory* (1968) that before the Enlightenment, anthropology did not really exist.

During the Enlightenment, a number of intellectuals used the philosophies of Newton and Locke to organize and analyze data on human diversity generated by the voyages of geographical discovery. One such intellectual was Jesuit Father Joseph Lafitau (1671-1746), who in *Customs of American Savages Compared with Those of Earliest Times* (1724) created an inventory of culture traits and categories considerably less **ethnocentric**, or culturally biased, than those of his **ethnocentric** predecessors. Lafitau was one of several Jesuit missionaries whose eighteenth-century accounts of native North Americans are still consulted by ethnohistorians. Another Enlightenment figure was French social reformer Jean Jacques Rousseau (1712-1778), who in *Discourse on the Origin and Foundation of Inequality among Men* (1751) speculated on how and why human differences had developed over time. Rousseau sought to counteract what he considered to be overly intellectualized Enlightenment formulations by emphasizing human pathos and emotion. His speculations led him to conclude in *The Social Contract* (1762) that humanity had been happier in the past, and that **noble savagery** was a condition whose disappearance ought to be **noble savagery** lamented. In their speculative reconstructions of the past, both Lafitau and Rousseau used living savages as models for past savages. This was an early application of what in nineteenth-century anthropology would be called the **comparative method**. **comparative method**

Aping the accomplishments of Newton, some Enlightenment intellectuals sought to discover "laws" of human history. These so-called **universal historians** proposed stages of human development **universal historians** during which, according to the philosophy of Locke, human experience was understood to have accumulated as culture. A prime example was Italian philosopher Giambattista Vico (1668-1744), who in *The New Science* (1725) described how humanity had passed through the three stages of Gods, heroes, and men. These stages were secular and, according to Vico, the product of human, not divine, action. Another universal historian was the Baron de la Brède et de Montesquieu (1689-1755), who in *The Spirit of Laws* (1748) attempted to show how rules governing human conduct have always been correlated with culture. More radical was French philosopher François Marie Arouet de Voltaire (1694-1778). In *Essay on the Customs and Spirit of Nations* (1745), Voltaire actively attacked the theological view of history and traced the growth of Christianity in secular terms. British historian Edward Gibbon (1737-1794) used the same approach more subtly in *The Decline and Fall of the Roman Empire* (1776-1778).

Some universal historians of the Enlightenment stand out as more recognizably anthropological than others. One was French statesman Anne Robert Jacques Turgot (1727-1781), who in *Plans for Two Discourses on Universal History* (1750) described the passage of humanity through the three stages of hunting, pastoralism, and farming. Another was French philosopher Marie Jean de Condorcet (1743-1794), who in *Outline of the Intellectual Progress of Mankind* (1795) added more stages, for a total of ten, the last of which Condorcet predicted to be the future. Prediction, he urged, was based on his confidence in laws about the past. Scottish historians Adam Ferguson (1728-1816), John Millar (1735-1801), and William Robertson (1721-1793) stressed the importance of technology and economy in defining stages of universal history. Robertson even used the schema **savagery, barbarism, and civilization**, which became commonplace in the nineteenth century. In fact, from the perspective of nineteenth-century anthropology, the Scottish Enlightenment appears more theoretically sophisticated than the French.

Enlightenment schemes of universal history were united by the common themes of human reason, progress, and perfectibility. Reason referred to the exercise of human intellect unfettered by authoritarian faith, including faith in religion. Progress referred to the resulting positive direction of historical change, opposite the direction presupposed by medieval Christianity, which considered humanity degenerate and fallen from the grace of God. Perfectibility referred to the final outcome of reason and progress which, according to Enlightenment thinkers, would lead to steady improvement of human conditions on Earth. Toward the end of the eighteenth century, these themes became slogans for social reform, then rallying cries for the French Revolution.

The Rise of Positivism

The French Revolution was a political movement that overthrew the absolute monarchy of the Bourbon regime and its associated system of upper-class privilege, unleashing a new middle class, the **bourgeoisie**. Beginning in 1789, the Revolution lasted for a protracted, bloody decade before Napoleon Bonaparte (1769-1821) assumed control of France in 1799. In a move widely considered to be a betrayal of revolutionary ideals, Bonaparte made himself Emperor and plunged France into a series of expansionist wars that lasted until he was defeated at the Battle of Waterloo in 1815. Afterward, all of Europe needed a rest from political turmoil.

    bourgeoisie

    The Revolution was fought on the basis of Enlightenment ideals of human reason, progress, and perfectibility. When the Revolution turned out badly, European intellectuals turned their backs on these ideals. The result was a rise in conservative attitudes aimed at maintaining, or regaining, the political status quo. Conservatism appeared in a number of guises. One guise was fundamentalist Christianity, which condemned social science as excessively materialistic, atheistic, and amoral. Many new Christian denominations developed, espousing "evangelical" or **pietistic** perspectives. In this new theology, Newton's clockmaker God was replaced by a God of divine intervention, miracles, and punishment for those who strayed from the teachings of the Bible and its latter-day interpreters. Elsewhere, citi-

    pietistic

zens fed up with radical "social engineering" established utopian, or visionary, socialist communities where they could live and do as they pleased. A strong reaction to Napoleon's vision of empire was nationalism, which promoted the ideology and mythology of particular peoples rather than a universal outlook on humankind. In Germany, which struggled to achieve nationhood, there was a revival of faith in predestination and a longing to return to past glory, resulting in a retreat from the idea of progress. This development had a noticeable *volksgeist* effect on German ethnology, which embraced the idea of *volksgeist*, or special spirit, of Germans. Another guise of conservatism was Romanticism, a movement in art, literature, and even science that glorified the idiosyncratic, non-rational, and emotional sides of human nature and denied the primacy of Cartesian thought. Finally, there was racism, which was linked to all other guises of conservatism and in the nineteenth century flourished.

Conservatism also affected social science, which developed during the Enlightenment when principles of Newtonian science were used to investigate social change. In the early nineteenth century, social scientists also felt that it was time to put more emphasis on stability. The result was the all-encompassing philosophy of Positivism.

Positivism   Positivism (with a capital "P") was the creation of French philosopher Auguste Comte (1798-1857), an intellectual descendant of Marie Jean de Condorcet through intermediary Claude Henri, Comte de Saint-Simon (1760-1825). Comte's views are contained in his multi-volume work *Course of Positive Philosophy* (1830-42), where he described how almost all branches of knowledge have passed through three stages: theological, metaphysical, and positive. According to Comte, in the theological stage, phenomena were explained in terms of deities; in the metaphysical stage, in terms of abstract concepts; and in the positive stage, in terms of other phenomena. Starting with astronomy and physics in the Scientific Revolution, the natural sciences had already passed through the theological and metaphysical stages to become positive, meaning truly scientific. The social sciences, however, lagged behind. It was Comte's job to help them catch up. The social sciences had already passed out of the theological stage, where social phenomena had been explained in terms of God during the Middle Ages, well into the metaphysical stage, where they had been explained in terms of the abstract concept of reason during the Enlightenment. Now, Comte urged, social science should enter the positive phase, in the post-Enlightenment nineteenth century.

In Comte's scheme, science involved the search for generalizations. In positive social science, these generalizations would be of two kinds. **Social dynamics** (named after a branch of physics) would search for generalizations about social change, while **social statics** (physics again) would search for generalizations about social stability. Comte maintained that the French Revolution had gone too far in attempting to promote dynamic change and that its excesses needed to be tempered with social statics. Together, social dynamics and social statics would offer a comprehensive scientific perspective on social phenomena.

As the creator of Positivism, Comte was one of the founding fathers of modern social science, in particular sociology, which was built on the foundation of his pronouncement that social phenomena are to be explained in their own terms. At the same time, **positivism** (with a small "p") underwent several philosophical transformations, so that by the middle of the twentieth century it had become synonymous with an outlook that promoted detached, value-free science as the model for social scientific inquiry. Anthropologists opposed to the scientific model cite positivism a source of theoretical misguidance.

Marxism

As the nineteenth century progressed, in the wake of the French Revolution, the middle classes of Europe prospered. Meanwhile, the working classes grew restless and agitated for reform. Where the Industrial Revolution took hold, mainly in Britain, radical intellectuals rallied to support the growing labour movement. The most radical support came from Karl Marx and Friedrich Engels, co-creators of the theory of **dialectical materialism**, commonly called **Marxism**. Marxism has had a profound effect on the real world of politics. It has also affected anthropology, not only for this reason but also because

social dynamics

social statics

positivism

dialectical materialism

Marxism

aspects of Marx's thought have been elaborated and formally incorporated within anthropological theory, even by anthropologists who are in no sense Marxist in their "allegiance."

Karl Marx (1818-1883) was born in Prussia, studied philosophy at the University of Berlin, then law at the University of Bonn. He became interested in the relationship between politics and economics, turning to the utopian variety of socialism in 1843. Early on, he decided that utopian socialism was ineffective and that, to become effective, socialism would have to be made "scientific." Friedrich Engels (1820-1895) was the son of a German textile manufacturer who spent several years in the English cities of Manchester and Liverpool as the agent of a textile firm. England had already experienced the undesirable effects of industrialization and was debating parliamentary measures to improve the poor conditions of urban workers. Engels analyzed these conditions in *The Condition of the Working-Class in England* (1844), then expanded his analysis in collaboration with Marx. The result was their landmark treatise *The Communist Manifesto* (1848).

The essential ingredients of dialectical materialism can be found in *The Communist Manifesto* and the much larger work *Capital* (1867). Marx and Engels began with the premise of **materialism**, meaning their belief that human existence determines human consciousness, contrasted with the idealist belief that human consciousness determines human existence. More specifically, they believed that human thoughts, actions, and institutions are determined by their relationship to the **means of production**, meaning how people make a living in the material world. This relationship is always changing, because the means of production are always changing as people change their adaptations to physical conditions. In prehistory, according to Marx and Engels, who drew this part of their analysis from contemporary anthropology, people lived in a socio-economic system with material goods belonging to all, no private property, and equality under the "law." In civilization, however, powerful individuals gained control of land, the basic source of wealth. Thus, **primitive communism** was superseded by a system of unequal classes and the exploitation of one class by another.

materialism

means of production

primitive communism

Marx and Engels maintained that all modern societies are based on class distinctions. These distinctions become institutionalized in church and state, which function to keep the **ruling class**, the class that controls the means of production, in power. As the means of production change, the nature of classes, which "organize" the means of production, also changes. Eventually, the means of production outgrow their form of organization, which is "overthrown" in a social revolution, from which a new social system emerges. In classical Marxism, the sequence of social revolutions is **dialectical**, according to a revised version of the philosophy of Georg Wilhelm Friedrich Hegel (1770–1831). Hegel, an extreme idealist, described a world spirit manifesting itself in history through dialectical transformations of the form **thesis-antithesis-synthesis**. The thesis came first, followed by its opposite, the anti-thesis, then followed by a combination of the thesis and antithesis, the synthesis. Marx and Engels were attracted to Hegel's philosophy but felt that it needed to be epistemologically up-ended. Therefore, they "stood Hegel on his head" and moved the dialectic from the ideal to the material world. In the resulting theory, dialectical materialism, social transformations assume a dialectical form, with one social stage, the thesis, inevitably "sowing the seeds of its own destruction" by harbouring its opposite, the antithesis, which manifests itself in social revolution. This stage is followed by a third social stage, the synthesis, that retains elements of the preceding two. Marx and Engels' main focus was materialism rather than dialectics. Their primary interest in revising Hegel's philosophy was to use it to explain what had happened in world history and, through a communist revolution, what would happen in the future.

Although Marx and Engels were aware of prehistory, ancient history, and non-Western history, they began their account with the Middle Ages and feudalism, a system of agricultural economics with classes consisting of ruling-class lords and a ruled-class of unfree labourers, the serfs. During feudal times, a new manufacturing class emerged, the capitalists, whose power rested on money rather than land. The capitalist means of production was manufacturing, which, because of what it could produce, was superior to agriculture

ruling class

dialectical

thesis-antithesis-synthesis

and eventually replaced it. For Marx and Engels, the triumph of capitalism over feudalism was the French Revolution, after which lords and serfs were superfluous and the new classes became the ruling-class bourgeoisie and a ruled-class of urban workers, the proletariat.

proletariat

Marx and Engels did not spend too much time analyzing feudalism and how it gave rise to capitalism. They were much more anxious to analyze capitalism and how it would give rise to communism. Their analysis was based on the labour theory of value, the materialist premise that goods and services should be valued in terms of the human labour required to produce them. According to this theory, the value of a good or service, a commodity, is directly related to the amount of labour put into it. Exploitation occurs when capitalists "expropriate" some of this value as profit. Moreover, capitalists buy and sell labour itself as a commodity, valuing it according to wages determined by the labour "market." The result is that workers are alienated from the product of their labour, and therefore from themselves.

labour theory of value

The disintegration of capitalism was the focus of the work *Capital*. In this work, Marx explained how at first capitalism was progressive, opening up new markets as an efficient way of producing goods. But capitalism became regressive. It became less efficient, as competition among manufacturers decreased and economic power was concentrated in fewer and fewer hands. The growth of monopolies was inevitable, Marx observed, because competition produced winners as well as losers. Soon the monopoly system outgrew the original capitalist system of product diversity. Rich monopolists got richer by increasing profits, and poor workers got poorer because profit was taken from their wages. The proletariat became pauperized, and, as small business people were squeezed out by competition, they swelled its ranks. Under free market conditions, a glut of labourers caused a decease in wages, intensifying poverty. Because of cheaper labour, profits increased. For a while, profits were reinvested in production, but eventually production generated more and more goods able to be bought by fewer and fewer people. This downward spiral of events led to economic recession, depression, and labour unrest. Soon the capitalist world was ripe for revolution.

In the mature phase of capitalism, the means of production would already be concentrated in a few locations. Workers could easily seize them in the name of the proletariat and nationalize them in the name of a nation governed by workers. The first stage of the revolution would be a temporary **dictatorship of the proletariat**, whose job would be to destroy the bourgeoisie as a class and eliminate private profit by putting it to public use. The result would be a classless society in which church and state, formerly serving the interests of a few capitalists, would become an agent of all workers. Eventually, the state would "wither away" and the final stage would emerge, the true stage of communism, in which workers would work according to their ability and receive compensation according to their needs. Final communism would represent a return to primitive communism with the technology of the industrial age.

Marxism achieved major political victories in the Soviet and Chinese revolutions of the twentieth century. These revolutions led to the installation of Marxist dogma and its modification by powerful politicians like Vladimir Lenin (1870-1924), Joseph Stalin (1879-1953), and Mao Tse-tung (1893-1976). Marxism also took root outside politics in academic disciplines like anthropology.

In the twentieth century, beginning in earnest in the 1930s, a small minority of anthropologists professed allegiance to one or more of the tenets of Marxism. Marxist anthropologists are diverse, but, except for **structural Marxists** of the 1970s and later, most of them stand on common intellectual ground. Few of them accept the entire theory of dialectical materialism, which history has helped refute. But they do demonstrate a personal commitment to help oppressed and disadvantaged people and are willing to use anthropology professionally for that purpose. Theoretically, they prefer materialist over idealist explanations of culture change and historical over ahistorical approaches to cultural analysis. In cultural analysis, they emphasize "class," because Marxism implies that different classes have different ideologies and "consciousnesses," often fundamentally opposed. In

dictatorship of the proletariat

structural Marxists

vulgar materialists Marxist circles, there are disputes between **vulgar materialists**, said by their detractors to be simple-minded materialists, and Marxist anthropologists who embrace one form or another of dialectics. This latter group includes the structural Marxists, who blend classical Marxism with the twentieth-century anthropology of French structuralist Claude Lévi-Strauss. Marxist anthropologists, vulgar and structural alike, join forces in criticizing anthropologists who promote "value-free" science — so-called positivist anthropologists. All science, they say, is value-laden, and those who deny this truth naively or maliciously perpetuate social inequities. In academic journals, at professional meetings and elsewhere, debates about Marxism in anthropology can be heated.

Classical Cultural Evolutionism

The word evolution means transformation of forms, a process in which something changes while remaining partially the same. Evolution is associated most closely with biology, but it can also apply to any natural or social science attempting to reconstruct the past. The Marxist theory of dialectical materialism and the Enlightenment schemes of universal history were evolutionary. So was the first major

classical cultural cultural anthropological "ism": **classical cultural evolutionism** of the
evolutionism nineteenth century.

Classical cultural evolutionism represents a continuation of Enlightenment universal historicism — with one important difference. While eighteenth-century universal historians concentrated on modern Western history, nineteenth-century cultural evolu-

prehistory tionists concentrated on the history of non-Western peoples in **prehistory**, the time before writing. This difference derived from expanded ethnographic understanding of aboriginal peoples and convincing new archaeological evidence that there *was* a prehistory. Taken together, ethnography and archaeology allowed nineteenth-century anthropologists to construct cultural evolutionary schemes in which descriptions of prehistoric artifacts were "fleshed out" with descriptions of present-day "primitive" peoples whose artifacts looked similar. This use of ethnography to supplement archaeology was called the "comparative method." In the early twentieth century, influential anthropologists criticized the comparative method as too speculative, and cultural evolutionism fell out of favour as an anthropological theory. In the late 1940s, it was revived by another group of anthropologists who called themselves **neo-evolutionists** and labelled their nineteenth-century predecessors "classical." neo-evolutionists

The heyday of classical cultural evolutionism was the period from the 1860s through the 1890s. Although this period followed publication of Charles Darwin's *Origin of Species* (1859), cultural evolutionism does *not* represent an application of Darwin's biological ideas to the realm of culture. Cultural evolutionists were far more interested in ethnography, archaeology, and an expanded view of universal history than in Darwin's theory of evolution by natural selection. It would be historically inaccurate to label cultural evolutionists "social" or "cultural" Darwinists.

Classical cultural evolutionists fall into "major" and "minor" categories. Major figures were more original, influential, and productive as authors. Minor figures published less, had less influence, and commented more on the ideas of others. The major classical cultural evolutionists were Herbert Spencer (1820-1903), John Lubbock (1834-1913), Lewis Henry Morgan (1818-1881), Edward Burnett Tylor (1832-1917), and James Frazer (1854-1941). Minor classical cultural evolutionists included Henry Maine (1822-1888), Johann Bachofen (1815-1887), and John McLennan (1827-1881). With the exception of Bachofen, a German, and Morgan, an American, all of them were British. The effect of their work was to reinforce the prevailing attitude of smug Victorian superiority by demonstrating how modern civilization had evolved from primitive cultures in the direction of "progress."

Classical cultural evolutionists were interested in an array of cultural institutions and beliefs. One group, led by Morgan, was interested in marriage, family, and sociopolitical organization. Another group, led by Tylor, was interested in religion, magic, and other ideological systems. With the exception of Spencer, a philosopher or sociologist

Sir James Frazer (1854-1941) The distinguished late-Victorian anthropologist sits in his armchair. [Reprinted by permission of Pitt Rivers Museum, University of Oxford, England.]

more than an anthropologist, and Lubbock, an archaeologist as much as a cultural anthropologist, the classical cultural evolutionists "specialized" in one or the other of these interest groups.

Lewis Henry Morgan, an unlikely candidate for future anthropological fame, grew up in and around Rochester, New York, where he later practised law. He belonged to a fraternal order known as the League of the Iroquois and, in order to authenticate the order's rituals, began to study nearby Iroquois tribes, eventually becoming adopted by the Iroquois and helping them press their native land-claims cases in court. In his studies, Morgan relied heavily on his bilingual native assistant Ely Parker (1823-1895), probably the first significant informant in the history of American ethnography. Morgan took a keen interest in kinship, the study of how people are related to one another formally. This interest led to his first major book, *League of the Ho-de-no-sau-nee, or Iroquois* (1851), a study of Iroquois social organization. He expanded his studies with information gathered from travels throughout the United States and Canada, and from responses to questionnaires distributed around the world by the Smithsonian Institution. This information was incorporated into his more comprehensive books, *Systems of Consanguinity and Affinity of the Human Family* (1870) and his magnum opus *Ancient Society* (1877).

In *Ancient Society* Morgan presented a vast scheme of cultural evolution on several interrelated levels. He began with the general stages of savagery, barbarism, and civilization, defined — somewhat inconsistently — as stages of hunting and gathering, plant and animal domestication, and "the state." Each of these stages was divided — again somewhat inconsistently — into substages of "lower," "middle," and "upper." Morgan recognized that there were two kinship types. The classificatory type lumped together kinship categories that Anglo-Americans split into two or more categories, using, for example, a single term for "brother" and "brother's children." The descriptive type, exemplified by Anglo-Americans, maintained such split categories. Morgan believed that the classificatory type of kinship had predominated during savagery and barbarism, then evolved into the descriptive type with the advent of civilization, when property superseded kinship as the main determinant of social relations. Groups still practising classificatory kinship were said to be carryovers from the savage or barbaric stage.

Morgan divided kinship types into kinship systems, beginning with the Malayan system, where "mother" and "father" were lumped with "mother" and "mother's brother." According to Morgan, the Malayan system evolved into the Turanian-Ganowanian, or Iroquois, system, when cross-cousins, cousins related through parents of the

Margin notes: informant · classificatory · descriptive · cross-cousins

opposite sex, became distinguished. Then, when social relations reckoned through descent superseded social relations based on distinctions between sex, there evolved **unilineal kinship systems** of sibs, clans, and tribes. At first, still in the stage of savagery, descent was reckoned through the female line, because, owing to pregnancy, female parenthood could be determined more reliably than male parenthood. In the stage of barbarism, however, kinship reckoning through the male line commenced, changing matrisibs, matriclans, and **matrilineal** tribes into patrisibs, patriclans, and **patrilineal** tribes. Male kinship became even more important in the stage of civilization. To all these stages, kinship types, and kinship systems, Morgan added family types, beginning with the **consanguine** type, based on group marriage between brothers and sisters, and evolving through a series of prohibitions of marriage between relatives into the monogamous nuclear family of civilized times.

[margin: unilineal kinship systems]

[margin: matrilineal]

[margin: patrilineal]

[margin: consanguine]

A pivotal part of Morgan's scheme was his belief that a fundamental cultural shift occurred in the transition from the prehistoric stage of barbarism into the stage of civilization, which Morgan characterized by writing, cities, monumental architecture, and other anthropological hallmarks of states (contrasted with bands, tribes, and chiefdoms). For Morgan, this shift occurred when, because of the demands of plant and animal domestication in cities, territorial relations became more important than kinship relations. The growth of private property at the expense of community property prompted certain privileged groups to retain private property by inheritance through the male line. This shift in turn led to the emergence of stratified social classes whose access to strategic material resources was unequal. According to Morgan, beginning in antiquity, the stage of civilization became fundamentally different from the preceding stages of savagery and barbarism. Moreover, like other cultural evolutionists, Morgan considered present-day primitive cultures to be vestiges of the prehistoric past.

When Karl Marx and Friedrich Engels read *Ancient Society*, they were excited to find in it anthropological support for their belief that class-based inequalities were not engrained in human nature and that, under certain circumstances, a more egalitarian political system could work. They set about using Morgan's scheme to augment the theory of dialectical materialism by showing how the institution of private property had originated and how, when it was abolished, the world would return, at least figuratively, to the communism with which humanity began. When Marx died, Engels completed the task. In his book *Origin of the Family, Private Property, and the State* (1884), Engels added Morgan to the select group of non-Marxists whose thoughts have been declared compatible with the Marxist cause.

Although partially "dated," the body of Morgan's work has endured, and most modern anthropologists consider him to be the father of kinship studies. His nineteenth-century contemporaries disputed certain points. Differences between Morgan and minor classical cultural evolutionists centred on the sequence of cultural stages and the causes of their transformations. Morgan proposed a general evolutionary sequence of group marriage, or marriage ungoverned by complex kinship, followed by kinship determined through matrilineal and patrilineal descent. In *Ancient Law* (1861), Henry Maine disagreed, arguing that the first form of family was patrilineal. Maine also added an evolutionary distinction between **status societies**, which were family-oriented, held property in common, and maintained social control by social sanctions, and **contract societies**, which stressed individualism, held property in private, and maintained social control by legal sanctions. In *Primitive Marriage* (1865), John McLennan agreed with Morgan that group marriage had preceded patrilineal descent but disagreed with him on how the transition from one to the other had occurred. According to McLennan, group marriage was a period of great struggle in which not everybody who was born could survive. This situation led to **female infanticide**, the preferential killing of female over male children. The resulting shortage of females meant that they had to share males as mates, leading to **polyandry**. Males also captured females from other groups, leading to **exogamy**, or "mating out." In *Mother Right* (1861), Johann Bachofen made similar arguments. Judged by modern standards, all of these schemes were excessively speculative, far beyond the ability of empirical evidence to determine.

status societies

contract societies

female infanticide

polyandry
exogamy

Morgan's British counterpart was Edward Burnett Tylor, the "father" of cultural anthropology in Britain and, some say, in the West.

armchair anthropologist Tylor was a prototypical Victorian **armchair anthropologist**, who based his evolutionary schemes on reason as much as on ethnographic and archaeological data. In reconstructing culture, he correlated cultural components, called **adhesions**, and looked for clues to the past in cultural vestiges, called **survivals**. He argued vigorously against the Christian idea of human degeneration, arguing instead in favour of the secular Victorian idea of human progress. Tylor is credited with a number of important anthropological "firsts." He became the first academic professor of anthropology, at Oxford University in 1884; wrote the first anthropology textbook, *Anthropology* (1881); and, in *Primitive Culture* (1871), offered the first definition of culture by a professional anthropologist — "[that] complex whole which includes knowledge, belief, art, law, morals, custom and any other capabilities and habits acquired by man as a member of society."

adhesions

survivals

Tylor's principal interest was the evolution of magico-religious beliefs and institutions, which he explained as the accumulation of rational answers to reasonable questions about the natural world. This approach was also taken by John Lubbock, who in *The Origin of Civilization* (1870) outlined a scheme for the evolution of magic and religion. Lubbock's scheme began with atheism, the belief in no deity, and ended with the belief in an omnipotent, or all-powerful, God. Evolutionary philosopher Herbert Spencer, author of *Principles of Sociology* (1876), took a similar approach to the evolution of magic and religion. A synthesis of Tylor's and Spencer's views can serve to illustrate the role of reason in this group of classical cultural evolutionists.

In the Tylor-Spencer synthesis, religion, or proto-religion, began when the earliest prehistoric people tried to solve natural puzzles. Prehistoric people might have observed, for example, that clouds appear and disappear and the sun rises and sets, while rocks fail to move. Why were some natural objects animated, others not? The answer was that animated objects possessed **anima**, an invisible and diffuse supernatural force. Organisms were particularly animated, so their anima must have been particularly strong. Human organisms

anima

were animated in curious ways. In dreams, for example, people experienced themselves in different places, then awoke to find themselves somewhere else. People cannot be physically present in more than one place at the same time, so, the reasoning went, they must have two dimensions, a physical dimension and a non-physical, or spiritual, dimension, which "travels." This spiritual dimension became the "soul." Observations on death served to confirm the existence of souls. When people die, initially they look the same as in life, but they are no longer animated. Therefore, their invisible souls must have departed. But where do souls go? Many never return, so they must gather in another world, the "afterlife." Other souls return to haunt and possess the living as "ghosts." Therefore, these ghost-souls, some good and others bad, must be able to **transmigrate**.

transmigrate

If souls survive after death, should they not be able to be contacted in life? In the Tylor-Spencer synthesis, contacting souls became the job of magico-religious specialists like sorcerers and **shamans**. Furthermore, in a non-literate and kin-based culture, souls would be reckoned as ancestors and venerated for their wisdom and advice, leading to **ancestor worship**. But how was the supernatural world of ancestral ghost-souls to be imagined? According to the synthesis, it could only be imagined as a reflection of life on earth, and, when culture evolved, images of the afterlife would evolve in tandem. For this reason, in prehistoric and primitive cultures, with multiple, equally-ranking lineages and clans, there would be multiple, equally-ranking ghost-souls revered as deities — **polytheism**. When, in civilization, culture became class-based and stratified, deities became ranked, and when, early in civilization, authority came to rest in the hands of a single pharaoh, emperor or priestly king, the number of deities shrank to one, for instance the omnipotent "King of Kings" of Christianity. In this way, "advanced" **monotheism**, the prevailing form of religion in Victorian Britain, was the end product of a series of cultural transformations starting with primitive animism at the beginning of prehistoric time — the idea of "progress."

shamans

ancestor worship

polytheism

monotheism

Evolution results in continuity as well as change. In biological evolution, *Homo sapiens* retains traits of ancestral species, including prehuman species with ape-like and monkey-like traits. For many people, the suggestion that humanity is even partially animalistic provokes a visceral, negative reaction. Likewise, in Victorian Britain, cultural evolutionists like Tylor and Spencer were criticized and became controversial when they suggested that Christianity, like the beliefs of people everywhere, had "primitive" roots. Anthropology has had a somewhat radical reputation ever since.

The remaining major classical cultural evolutionist was James Frazer, whose multi-volume work *The Golden Bough* (1890) was a cross-cultural compendium of myths, folklore, and literature. Like Tylor, Frazer was interested in the evolution of the mental processes involved in magic, religion — and science. In his evolutionary scheme, magic came first and was based on the principles of contact and **sympathetic magic**. Magicians believed that they could control nature by bringing special elements together or, where direct contact was impossible, by substituting a concordant element. When magic failed, as Frazer knew it usually would, magicians turned to religion, distinguished by a sense of humility and acceptance that people cannot control nature, but can only *ask* for divine intervention through prayer and other acts of supplication. Finally, as "correct" knowledge of the world increased, religion was supplanted by science, which, like magic, exerted control over nature, but control that worked. Like monotheism for Tylor, science for Frazer represented the mature stage of a cultural evolutionary sequence that retained features of ancestral stages. The present was a product of the past, and thus seemingly trivial, exotic, and irrelevant aspects of culture made sense.

sympathetic magic

Evolutionism vs. Diffusionism

Classical cultural evolutionists embraced the nineteenth-century doctrine of **psychic unity**, formulated by German geographer and ethnographer Adolf Bastian (1826-1905). According to this doctrine, all peoples, primitive and civilized alike, had the same basic capacity for cultural change. Primitive peoples were less advanced than civilized peoples not because their primitiveness was innate, but because they

psychic unity

had been stunted in evolutionary growth through contact with other peoples or simply because they had started evolving later. The doctrine of psychic unity represented a continuation of the eighteenth-century Enlightenment belief that all peoples could progress.

Related to psychic unity was the doctrine of **independent invention**, an expression of faith that all peoples could be culturally creative. According to this doctrine, different peoples, given the same opportunity, could devise the same idea or artifact independently, without external stimulus or contact. Independent invention was one explanation of cultural change. The contrasting explanation was **diffusionism**, the doctrine that inventions arise only once and can be acquired by other groups only through borrowing or migration. Diffusionism was non-egalitarian, because it presupposed that some peoples were culturally creative while others could only copy. When cultural evolutionism fell out of favour in the early twentieth century, diffusionism was there to take its place. independent invention diffusionism

A simple diffusionist concept was **culture area**, introduced by American anthropologist Clark Wissler (1870-1947) in 1917. Motivated by New World pride, Wissler wanted to show European anthropologists that American Indian groups were not all the same. Therefore, he divided Indian groups into distinct culture areas, each with a centre where the most important traits of the group originated, and from which they had outwardly diffused. Following Wissler's lead, other American Indianists used the culture area concept to organize data, catalogue artifacts, and arrange museum displays. culture area

European versions of diffusionism were much more theoretically extreme. One notorious version was **heliocentrism**, promulgated by British and British Commonwealth anthropologists Grafton Elliot Smith (1871-1937), William Perry (1887-1949), and, for some of his career, William H. R. Rivers (1864-1922). Smith and his fellow theoreticians were fascinated by stone megaliths like Egyptian pyramids, which they linked to a cult of sun worship. Citing similarities between pyramids and stone megaliths in Europe and Central and South America, Smith pronounced that world civilization had originated around 4000 B.C. in Egypt, then spread out, becoming more heliocentrism

Culture Areas of North America. The culture area concept facilitated American anthropological investigations throughout the twentieth century.

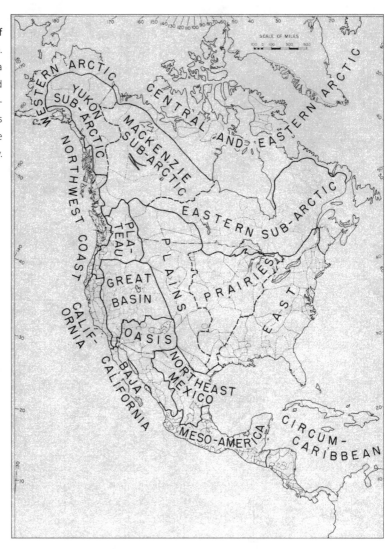

"dilute" and in some places never taking hold because natives were incapable of assimilation. Smith converted Rivers and Perry, whose book *The Children of the Sun* (1923) became a staple of this theoretical trade.

Another extreme version of diffusionism was the *kulturkreis*, or culture circle, school, derived in part from the anthropo-geography of German ethnologist Friedrich Ratzel (1844-1904). Interested in the relationship of people to their geographical neighbours, anthropo-geographers expressed strong opposition to Adolf Bastian's doctrine of psychic unity. Ratzel believed that, after diffusion, culture traits could undergo adaptations to local conditions, masking their sources. To overcome this obstacle, he invoked the criterion of form, which implied that similar and functionally useless traits were the ones that had probably diffused. Ratzel's follower Leo Frobenius (1873-1938) used geographical statistics to explore patterns of diffusion further. The criterion of form and geographical statistics both figured in the *kulturkreis* approach of Fritz Graebner (1877-1934) and Wilhelm Schmidt (1868-1954). In *The Method of Ethnology* (1911), Graebner argued that primitive bands with seminal ideas had spread around the world in a complex pattern of overlapping and interacting concentric circles. In *On the Origin of the Idea of God* (1926-1955), Schmidt described how, through diffusion, the seminal idea of monotheism had "degenerated."

Heliocentrism and the *kulturkreis* approach appealed to certain archaeologists as well as cultural anthropologists. An undercurrent of both approaches was the hereditarian belief that some human races were more capable of cultural innovation than others. Hereditarianism, or "racism," was an attitude that early twentieth-century anthropologists strongly opposed. As a result, doctrinaire diffusionism never achieved a wide following and, especially after National Socialism (i.e., Nazism), faded from mainstream theoretical view.

kulturkreis

culture circle

anthropo-geography

criterion of form

Archaeology Comes of Age

Archaeology, the study of past material culture, arose during the Renaissance, when scholars began to study classical artifacts to supplement what they could learn from classical texts. During the Enlightenment, archaeology continued to be the handmaiden of history, even though in northern Europe written records of the past were much more scant. An autonomous archaeology required that artifacts be the *only* kind of evidence of the past. This requirement could be met only after acceptance of the existence of "pre-"history.

The scientific community began to accept the existence of prehistory toward the middle of the nineteenth century. This acceptance was built on decades of preceding archaeological work. The first significant archaeological chronology independent of written records was the **Three Age System** of Christian Thomsen (1788-1865). Thomsen was a Danish museum curator who organized artifacts into the sequence of Stone, Bronze, and Iron ages, then subdivided these ages **seriationally**, according to the evolution of artifact style. He implemented his chronology in the Museum of Northern Antiquities in Copenhagen and incorporated it into his influential *Guidebook to Scandinavian Antiquity* (1836). Fellow countryman Jens J.A. Worsaae (1821-1885) continued Thomsen's work by investigating the **stratigraphy**, or systematic layering, of artifacts in Danish shell middens. In *The Primeval Antiquities of Denmark* (1843), Worsaae generalized the Three Age System to most of Europe. Daniel Wilson (1816-1892), a British archaeologist who later emigrated to Canada, employed the Three Age System in *The Archaeology and Prehistoric Annals of Scotland* (1851); it was Wilson who actually coined the term "prehistory." In the 1850s, archaeological examination of ancient dwellings on lake shores in Switzerland showed that the late **Stone Age** of Europe had seen plant and animal domestication. To designate this new phase of agriculture and animal husbandry, archaeologists added **Neolithic**, or **New Stone Age**, to their chronologies.

These early archaeological chronologies had to fit within the relatively brief time span of approximately 6,000 years, which is how

Grave Creek Burial Mound, West Virginia
Proponents of the nineteenth-century "Moundbuilder Myth" refused to believe that mounds like this one, depicted here by an artist, could have been constructed by American Indians or their ancestors.

long most Christian scientists believed that human beings had been living on earth. In order to make prehistory longer, new archaeological evidence was required. This evidence came from Stone Age caves and glacial deposits on river terraces in Britain and France. The key finds here were human skeletal remains and stone tools in geological association with skeletal remains of extinct prehistoric animals, mainly mammoth and woolly rhinoceros. These finds conflicted with fundamentalist Christianity, because the fundamentalist, or literal, interpretation of the Bible was that God had created human beings *after* other forms of life. Non-fundamentalist Christians were more inclined to accept this new archaeological evidence and the longer period of prehistory it implied. In 1859, British geologist Charles Lyell (1797-1875) led a contingent of distinguished scientists to the Somme River Valley in northern France, where amateur archaeologist Jacques Boucher de Crèvecoeur de Perthes (1788-1868) had discovered a series of old Stone Age tools. The contingent pronounced the tools authentic. Their action marked the first scientific consensus about the great time depth of prehistory and is the symbolic birth of the science of prehistoric archaeology.

This action spurred more prehistoric archaeological research that was incorporated into major syntheses like Lyell's *The Geological Evidence of the Antiquity of Man* (1863) and *Pre-Historic Times* (1865) by Paleolithic John Lubbock, who coined the term **Paleolithic**, or **Old Stone Age**. Well Old Stone Age before the end of the century, archaeologists had established a detailed chronology of the Paleolithic and all other major stages of European prehistory.

Like cultural evolutionists, archaeologists used the comparative method to reconstruct the prehistoric past. A prime example was Lubbock, whose 1865 book was fully titled *Pre-Historic Times, as Illustrated by Ancient Remains, and the Manner and Customs of Modern Savages*. But prehistoric archaeologists were less generous than cultural evolutionists in granting modern "savages" the ability to progress. Lubbock believed that white Europeans were the prime beneficiaries of a material progress that had been achieved through millennia of human struggle. In *A History of Archaeological Thought* (1989), Bruce The Imperial Synthesis Trigger represents Lubbock's attitude as **The Imperial Synthesis** and characterizes it as racist rationalization for European colonial expansion. Racism was certainly widespread, because outside Europe, where the prehistoric past was not "white," the accomplishments of prehistoric races were denigrated. In North America, archaeologists were loath to accept the idea that Indians could have built the complex earthen mounds found along the Mississippi River valley. Moundbuilder Myth Instead, they proposed the **Moundbuilder Myth**. According to this myth, these mounds had been built by a pre-Indian race that either had migrated to Central and South America to build the grand monuments of Aztec and Incas or had "degenerated" into Indians. A cornerstone publication on this controversy was *Ancient Monuments of the Mississippi Valley* (1848) by Ephraim G. Squier (1821-1888) and Edwin H. Davis (1811-1888). The same racist attitude prevailed in Africa, where archaeologists attributed mysterious stone ruins to King Solomon or other ancient Near Easterners. British colonial capitalist Cecil Rhodes (1853-1902) embraced this opinion and used it to argue that, in colonizing former Rhodesia, Europeans were really reclaiming lands that were formerly white. Colonialist archaeology came into play almost everywhere European archaeologists encountered non-white native peoples. Racism was endemic in nineteenth-century anthropology.

Darwinism

The racism of nineteenth-century anthropology was linked to the smug optimism and sense of superiority of Victorian times. Darwinism, the name given to ideas associated with Charles Darwin's theory of biological evolution, was part cause and part effect of these Victorian attitudes. The long, complex story of Darwinism begins with the Scientific Revolution.

Darwinism

While dynamic, the universe envisioned by Isaac Newton was not evolving. Bodies moving according to the law of universal gravitation were not being transformed into *new* bodies or arranged in new ways. Evolution, however, was a logical next step. The first Newtonian-era scientists to explore evolution were geologists interested in the origin and development of the Earth. In medieval cosmologies, the Earth was "special" because it was the centre of the universe and the habitat of people, the most noble creation of God. In the seventeenth century, such views persisted, so geology had to be carefully reconciled with Scripture. One reconciliation was attempted by Thomas Burnet (1635-1715) in *The Sacred Theory of the Earth* (1691). According to Burnet, after Creation, the Earth had cooled, and layers of land formed above seas. The shape of the Earth was a perfect circle, created for people who then sinned and had to be punished. Punishment took the form of a deluge, or global flood, that caused almost all land to collapse under water, leaving "ugly," imperfectly-shaped mountains as a reminder of this sin. Another reconciliation was attempted by William Whiston (1667-1752) in *A New Theory of the Earth* (1696). According to Whiston, after Creation, a comet had passed Earth and distributed dust that solidified into land by the force of gravity. Later, another comet distributed drops of water that precipitated the

Carolus Linnaeus'
Biological Classification
of Humanity.

In *Systema Naturae*
(1735), Linnaeus (1707-
1778) was one of the
first naturalists to classify
the genus *Homo* in the
animal kingdom.

MAMMALIA.

ORDER I. PRIMATES.

Fore-teeth cutting; upper 4, parallel; teats 2 pectoral.

1. HOMO.

Sapiens. Diurnal; varying by education and fituation.

2. Four-footed, mute, hairy. *Wild Man.*

3. Copper-coloured, choleric, erect. *American.*

Hair black, ftraight, thick; *noftrils* wide, *face* harfh; *beard* fcanty; *obftinate*; content free. *Paints* himfelf with fine red lines. *Regulated* by cuftoms.

4. Fair, fanguine, brawny. *European.*

Hair yellow, brown, flowing; *eyes* blue; *gentle*, acute, inventive. *Covered* with clofe veftments. *Governed* by laws.

5. Sooty, melancholy, rigid. *Afiatic.*

Hair black; *eyes* dark; *fevere*, haughty, covetous. *Covered* with loofe garments. *Governed* by opinions.

6. Black, phlegmatic, relaxed. *African.*

Hair black, frizzled; *fkin* filky; *nofe* flat; *lips* tumid; *crafty*, indolent, negligent. *Anoints* himfelf with greafe. *Governed* by caprice.

Monftrofus Varying by climate or art.

1. Small, active, timid. *Mountaineer.*
2. Large, indolent. *Patagonian.*
3. Lefs fertile. *Hottentot.*
4. Beardlefs. *American.*
5. Head conic. *Chinefe.*
6. Head flattened. *Canadian.*

The anatomical, phyfiological, natural, moral, civil and focial hiftories of man, are beft defcribed by their refpective writers.

Vol. I.—C   2. SIMIA.

Biblical Flood. Both Whiston's and Burnet's reconciliations were theologically ominous, because they implied that Earth was very old and rendered constant divine intervention redundant.

Meanwhile, as faith in science began to supplant faith in Christianity, a pressing problem arose. Geologists discovered fossils of marine forms of life embedded in sedimentary rocks formed underwater but currently far above water on land. How did these fossils get there? Answering this question was a preoccupation of eighteenth-century geology. An initial explanation was that the rocks were products of geological destruction, dislocation, and receding waters of the Biblical Flood. It soon became apparent, however, that marine fossil-bearing strata were far more geologically complex. There were two options: either water had receded, or land had risen. Geologists who preferred the first option were called **Neptunists**, named after Neptune, the Roman god of the sea; those who preferred the second option were called **Vulcanists**, named after Vulcan, the Roman god of fire. Pursuing the initial explanation, Neptunists maintained that marine fossils were deposited in sedimentary rocks formed underwater and then exposed as water receded. Vulcanists also believed that sedimentary rocks were formed underwater, but they maintained that the rocks were then thrust above water by earthquakes and volcanoes caused by pressure from a hot, molten subterranean earthly core. When Vulcanists asked Neptunists where all the water went, Neptunists had no answer. But until there was more geological evidence of the power of earthquakes and volcanoes, Vulcanists were vulnerable too.

A convincing, essentially Vulcanist geology was finally achieved by James Hutton (1726-1797) in *Theory of the Earth* (1795), later popularized by John Playfair (1748-1819) in *Illustrations of the Huttonian Theory of the Earth* (1802). In the Hutton-Playfair model, not all sedimentary rocks were formed in universal water. Some debris washed into water from land, while molten masses penetrated the ocean floor and deposited additional strata, then thrust above water by volcanoes. These geological processes had been operating for so long that the

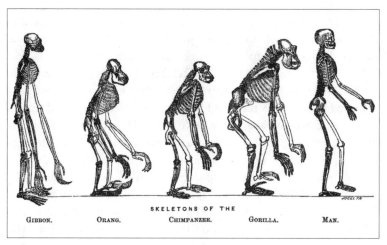

Comparison of Ape and Human Skeletons. By comparing the skeletons of apes and "man," Thomas H. Huxley (1825-1895) marshalled circumstantial evidence for human evolution.

SKELETONS OF THE

GIBBON.   ORANG.   CHIMPANZEE.   GORILLA.   MAN.

age of the Earth was almost beyond scientific comprehension. Hutton summarized his view of relentless geological activity as "no vestige of a beginning, no prospect of an end."

All these developments culminated in Charles Lyell's landmark multi-volume work *Principles of Geology* (1830-1833), a foundation of modern geology. To account for geological change, Lyell invoked a combination of agents, some Neptunist and others Vulcanist, that worked slowly over long periods of time. Because present-day agents of change like wind and water erosion were slow, yet the changes they had produced were dramatic, Lyell was forced to conclude that the Earth was extremely old. His geology was a brand of **uniformitarianism**, the doctrine that the same, nondramatic agents of geological change have been operating throughout history. Uniformitarianism contrasts with **catastrophism**, the doctrine that agents of geological change have been more dramatic in the past than in the present. Conservative Christian scientists who believed that the Earth was extremely young favoured catastrophism over uniformitarianism, because dramatic geological agents like global floods could produce major change quickly. A distinguished catastrophist, and antagonist of Lyell, was French paleontologist Georges Cuvier (1769-1832), who

uniformitarianism

catastrophism

interpreted change in the fossil record as evidence of a series of mass near-extinctions interspersed with survivals of a few fortunate life forms. Cuvier's catastrophism was "progressive," because it involved positive directional change. But Cuvier was not an evolutionist, because change for him was essentially discontinuous, without transformation. Lyell's uniformitarianism was less progressive, because, like his predecessor Hutton, he regarded constructive and destructive agents as counterbalancing, in the long run achieving equilibrium. Lyell was a geological evolutionist, however, because his geological agents caused transformational change. And while Lyell opposed uniformitarianism in biology, the great achievement of his friend Charles Darwin was to combine the transformism of uniformitarianism with the progressivism of catastrophism into a comprehensive theory of biological evolution.

In the history of the idea of biological evolution, the great debate was about the origin of species. A **species** is a group of plants or animals whose members can reproduce with one another but cannot reproduce with members of other species. Where do species come from? The traditional scientific answer, based on Christianity, was that God created all species, which were immutable, or fixed. New species did not appear in Creation through evolution, and old species did not disappear through extinction. Moreover, species were arranged in a fixed linear hierarchy, constructed by medieval philosophers as the **Great Chain of Being**. Traditionally, species were "real," not merely names for groups of individuals. They were transcendental, Platonic essences attesting to the perfection of Creation. A prime example of traditional creationism was Carolus Linnaeus (1707-1778), the Swedish biologist who classified living things into a hierarchy of taxonomic categories, using a system of **binomial nomenclature**, or two names, for the category of species. In his *System of Nature* (1735), Linnaeus introduced many of the taxonomic names (of kingdoms, phyla, genera, and so forth) that are used in evolutionary biology today. Until late in his life, however, Linnaeus denied evolution and adhered strongly to the creationist position.

More liberal, or radical, Enlightenment biologists broke rank with

species

Great Chain of Being

binomial nomenclature

traditional creationists. Their answer to the question of the origin of species was that species were created by nature and were mutable, or susceptible to change. New species appeared and disappeared through natural causes. Species were not necessarily arranged in a fixed linear hierarchy, and they were not "real" in the Platonic sense of the term. Instead, they were transient categories that altered the face of Creation. Biologists who adhered to this set of ideas were called transformists, developmentalists or, later, evolutionists.

Before Darwin, a number of scientists proposed theories of biological evolution, among them Georges-Louis Leclerc, Comte de Buffon (1707-1778) and Darwin's own grandfather, Erasmus Darwin (1731-1802). The most influential pre-Darwinian evolutionist was Jean-Baptiste Pierre Antoine de Monet Lamarck (1744-1829), whose *Zoological Philosophy* (1809) appeared exactly 50 years before Darwin's *Origin of Species* (1859). Lamarck's approach to evolution was different from Darwin's approach in ways that can be illustrated by an example of the evolution of the long-necked giraffe. According to Lamarck, the ancestor of the long-necked giraffe was a giraffe with a short neck. These short-necked giraffes lived on savannah-like grasslands where desirable edible vegetation was available on trees. To reach this vegetation, the giraffes stretched their necks. As a result, their offspring were born with longer necks, that is, necks longer than they would have been if their parents had not stretched. This new generation of giraffes stretched *their* necks for the same reason, so *their* offspring were born with longer necks still. Over time, as this process continued, neck length increased, until the present-day long-necked giraffe evolved. Lamarck was unable to *prove* that ancestral and descendant giraffes belonged to different species, because, with ancestral giraffes extinct, he was unable to demonstrate that members of the two groups could not reproduce. Nonetheless, by comparing the magnitude of their difference to the magnitude of differences among known species, he was able to render this judgment.

The non-Darwinian feature of Lamarckian evolution illustrated in this example will be obvious to any student of modern biology. It is the feature known as **inheritance of acquired characteristics**. In the exam-

inheritance of acquired characteristics

ple, the characteristic of longer necks was inherited by offspring because it was acquired by parents. Modern biologists have shown that acquired characteristics are not inherited unless their acquisition itself is hereditary, or pre-programmed in deoxyribonucleic acid, **DNA**. Except for recombination, DNA is inherited from generation to generation intact. Other non-Darwinian features of Lamarckian evolution, not illustrated in this example, are **vitalism**, the doctrine that evolution is self-motivated, or willed; **teleology**, the doctrine that evolution adheres to a long-range purpose or goal; and **orthogenesis**, the doctrine that evolution has worked in a straight line to produce *Homo sapiens*. From many moral points of view, these features make Lamarckian evolution more palatable than Darwinian evolution. In the early nineteenth century, when Darwin was growing up, the Lamarckian version of evolution was the one most commonly discussed.

DNA

vitalism

teleology

orthogenesis

Charles Darwin (1809-1882) grew up in England at the dawn of the Victorian era. As a young man, he wanted to study medicine, but he soon learned that he could not stand the sight of blood, so he dropped out of medical school in Edinburgh and enrolled in Christ's College, Cambridge. At Cambridge, he became a budding naturalist and was encouraged by a number of faculty "mentors." One mentor helped arrange his appointment as naturalist on the ship *H.M.S. Beagle*, which in 1831 set out on a five-year voyage around the world. The voyage of the *Beagle* was a crucible for Darwin's ideas.

Before the *Beagle* left England, Darwin had begun reading Lyell's *Principles of Geology*. During the voyage, he completed reading this work and became inspired to search for a biological process equivalent to uniformitarian processes in geology. As the *Beagle* sailed around the Atlantic and Pacific coasts of South America, Darwin observed that the geographical distribution of varieties of plants and animals correlated with the distribution of variation in useful environmental resources. When he visited the Galapagos Islands off the coast of Ecuador, he observed that varieties of finches and tortoises differed slightly from one island to another, and also differed from varieties on the South American mainland. How and why did these differences develop?

When the *Beagle* arrived back in England, Darwin was already converted to the idea of evolution. He undertook years of scientific research to strengthen his reputation as a naturalist while he pondered new, non-Lamarckian mechanisms that might make evolution work. Then he read *An Essay on the Principle of Population* (1798) by Thomas Robert Malthus (1766-1834). Malthus was the pessimistic political theorist who explained how the human population of the world was increasing geometrically (2, 4, 8, 16, 32, etc.) while global resources needed for human survival were increasing only arithmetically (2, 4, 6, 8, 10, etc.). The inevitable consequence of these trends was that not everyone born could possibly survive. Darwin embraced this Malthusian vision and broadened it to include all of biological nature, where organisms engage in a **struggle for existence** producing **survival of the fittest.**

struggle for existence

survival of the fittest

Knowing now how evolution worked, Darwin began to draft his book on evolution. He worked on the book off and on for many years until in 1858 he received a letter from fellow naturalist Alfred Russel Wallace (1823-1913). Wallace, writing from the Pacific South Seas, described a theory of evolution by **natural selection** that Darwin recognized immediately as almost exactly like his own. After consulting with friends, he decided to finish his book quickly. First, however, Darwin and Wallace presented a joint paper on evolution to a meeting of the Linnaean Society in London (neither man was actually there). The following year, in 1859, Darwin's *Origin of Species* appeared. Ever since, the theory of evolution by natural selection, independently formulated by both Darwin and Wallace, has been known as "Darwinism."

natural selection

A good way to understand Darwin's theory of evolution is to contrast it with Lamarck's theory using the example of the long-necked giraffe. Darwin would have approached this example with a different premise. A group, or population, of ancestral short-necked giraffes was living on savannah-like grasslands. They needed to eat vegetation from trees to survive. Some giraffes had slightly longer necks than others. These giraffes had a slight advantage over the other giraffes in the competitive struggle for vegetation needed to survive. Beating out the competition because of this natural advantage, they ate more, became healthier or in some other way had more offspring. Gradually, over time, as the longer-necked giraffes had more offspring than the shorter-necked giraffes, average neck length in the population increased, until the present long-necked giraffe species evolved.

Darwin represented this sequence of events as "natural selection," meaning, metaphorically, that "nature" selects advantageous traits just like human breeders "artificially" select advantageous traits when they domesticate plants and animals. The result in both cases is that organisms become adapted to their environments. To argue his case in *Origin of Species*, Darwin adduced several kinds of evidence. Except for the results of plant and animal breeding, almost all of this evidence was circumstantial. He argued that anatomical and embryological similarities among organisms, the presence of vestigial organs and, although incomplete, the record of fossils were all consistent with his theory. A problem for Darwinism — then and now — is that this same evidence is consistent with many versions of **creationism**. Suffice creationism it to say that eventually the scientific community came to accept Darwin's theory. His theory represents an extension of the Scientific Revolution from astronomy and physics into biology. Darwin really went *beyond* Newton, because he showed that basic structures of the universe evolve.

Origin of Species provoked a barrage of moral, religious, and social criticism. Many critics failed to realize, or admit, that the book made hardly any reference to the evolution of *Homo sapiens*. Darwin ducked this controversial topic for several years. Some of his friends, however, confronted the controversy head on. The main implication for *Homo sapiens* was the evolution of human mental and moral qualities. Most Christians believed that animals lacked spirituality and were, mentally and morally, a world apart from human beings. Could evolution bridge this gap? In *The Geological Evidence of the Antiquity of Man* (1863), Charles Lyell described human evolution as a natural leap onto a new plane of life. Alfred Russel Wallace disagreed, arguing that

Charles Darwin's Study at Down House, Kent, England. Darwin (1809-1882) wrote *Origin of Species* and other books here.

mental and moral superiority would have conferred no real selective advantage on animals and therefore could not have evolved in the first place. Why, for example, would an animal *need* to be artistic, mathematical or philosophical? According to Wallace, divine intervention must have been responsible. Other scientists were more open to the idea of Darwinian human evolution. At the time, only a few human fossils were known, and, unfortunately for human evolutionists, these fossils appeared neither particularly old nor particularly primitive. Still, in *Evidence as to Man's Place in Nature* (1863), Thomas Henry Huxley (1825-1895) — nicknamed "Darwin's Bulldog" because he defended Darwin so staunchly in public debates — classified people and apes in the same taxonomic order. Without fossils, the artifact record of prehistory became more important, so human evolutionists also cited the work of archaeologists like John Lubbock and cultural evolutionists like Lewis Henry Morgan and Edward Burnett Tylor.

Darwin eventually published his views on human evolution in *The Descent of Man* (1871). Much of this book, and also of Darwin's *The Expression of the Emotions in Man and the Animals* (1872), was devoted to the argument that differences between animals and people are differences in degree rather than in kind. To explain the evolution of human physical traits, Darwin used the mechanism of **sexual selection**. With sexual selection, traits evolve not because they confer an adaptive advantage in the struggle for existence, but because they make members of one sex more attractive to the other and in this way increase reproductive success. Human intelligence, Darwin said, *was* evolved by natural selection, as a by-product of upright stature, which freed human hands for the use of tools. To explain the evolution of human morality, Darwin relied on the mechanism of **group selection**. According to Darwin, the core of morality was **altruism**, the willingness to sacrifice oneself for the good of others. Altruism, he said, was initially selected in groups, when one member behaved altruistically and, as a result, other groups members benefitted. Later, after human beings became intelligent, they extended altruism beyond the local group to all humanity in the form of abstract moral codes.

sexual selection

group selection
altruism

Viewed from the perspective of modern science, Darwin's explanations appear to conflate, or confuse, biological and cultural evolution. In this regard, Darwin was not much different from his Victorian scientist contemporaries. Almost all nineteenth-century human evolutionists were extremely hereditarian. Like "racism" in archaeology, racism in biological anthropology was a legacy from the nineteenth century.

Darwin and his friends did not espouse many of the religious, moral, and social attitudes now labelled "Darwinian." The main religious challenge to Darwin was not based on Biblical fundamentalism, because by the 1860s the Bible was no longer widely accepted as necessarily historically accurate. The main religious challenge was based on morality. If human beings were the product of evolution, not divine creation, would not a system of morality have to be based on the process of evolution itself? And if so, would not the easiest way to construct such a system be to treat evolution as intrinsically and ultimately purposeful? The problem was that, contrasted with Lamarckian evolution, Darwinian evolution appeared to lack ultimate purpose and instead operated opportunistically, selecting characteristics adapted to only a circumscribed time and place. Alternatively, if Darwinian evolution were a divine instrument — God's way of creating — the mechanism of natural selection appeared excessively brutal. It involved relentlessly harsh struggle, competition, and death for individuals unable to adapt. It was always possible, of course, to argue, as many Darwinians did, that these unfortunate losses were compensated for by evolutionary "winners," who helped humanity "improve." But this position was morally precarious, and in most cases it was easier to abandon Darwinian evolution in favour of the Lamarckian mechanism of inheritance of acquired characteristics, which seemed more humane and offered hope that people might take charge of their evolutionary fate. In the late nineteenth century, **Lamarckism** became the doctrine of choice for the majority of scientists seeking to reconcile evolution with religious morality.

Lamarckism

Social Darwinism

synthetic philosophy

In discussions of social morality, the term **Social Darwinism** is historically misleading. Most of the social attitudes denoted by this term derive not from Darwin, but from Herbert Spencer, the most philosophical and sociological of the classical cultural evolutionists. Spencer promoted a grandiose **synthetic philosophy** based on the premise that homogeneity was evolving into heterogeneity in several universal domains. Referring to the domain of evolutionary biology, Spencer was Lamarckian rather than Darwinian, but referring to the domain of *social* evolution, he believed that vigorous individual enterprise had risen to the fore. According to Spencer, a system of individuals acting in their own self-interest produced the maximum social good. There were no moral absolutes. Instead, "might" made "right." Spencer believed that human evolution should be allowed to take its "natural" course, unfettered by interventions that would "artificially" bolster human weaknesses otherwise slated for defeat.

Spencer's was the most popular version of Social Darwinism and the one used most often to rationalize social inequities among races, classes, and genders. Meanwhile, Huxley, Darwin's "bulldog," advocated an opposing version. Huxley was an agnostic who actively doubted religion and believed that science should maintain moral neutrality. He opposed Spencer and anyone else who based social morality on biological evolution. To the contrary, argued Huxley, through cos-mic accident *Homo sapiens* has evolved to the point where people are able to understand that evolution has *no* purpose. Why not take advantage of this opportunity and create a morality that is indepen-dent of evolution and even goes *against* the harshness of nature? In the nineteenth century, between the extremes of Huxley and Spencer, there were so many different versions of Social Darwinism that the term really needs to be defined almost every time it is used.

Amidst all the wrangling over religious and social morality, Darwin's theory of evolution by natural selection suffered major scientific setbacks. From the beginning, there had not been much experimental proof that natural selection could produce new species, even with artificial breeding, which produced mainly subspecies, or varieties. Another problem was the fossil record. Darwin admitted that the record was imperfect and contained gaps, or **missing links**. Some scientists filled these gaps with speculative evolutionary sequences, such as those based on the **biogenetic law**. This law stated that **ontoge-ny**, the growth of an individual, recapitulated **phylogeny**, the evolu-tionary growth of a species. Proponents of the law made extreme statements about embryological and paleontological similarities and detracted from the credibility of evolution as empirical science. Yet another problem was the age of the Earth. Evolution by natural selec-tion was a slow process that required a great deal of time to account for changes observable in the fossil record. Contemporary physicists, thinking about volcanic activity as an agent of geological change, decided that the Earth had been much hotter in the past than in the present and that volcanic activity had been much more forceful. A troubling implication was that this volcanic activity had wrought geo-logical changes too quickly for Darwinian evolution to have worked. A final problem for Darwin was the **swamping effect**, the name given to the observation that small variations serving as raw material for natural selection would always be "swamped out" through heredity, preventing natural selection from ever getting started. Darwin was aware of all these scientific problems and as a result grew discouraged. He lost confidence in the complete efficacy of natural selection and,

missing links

biogenetic law
ontogeny
phylogeny

swamping effect

in later editions of *Origin of Species*, turned to other evolutionary mechanisms, including the Lamarckian mechanism of inheritance of acquired characteristics.

The solutions to Darwin's scientific problems were beyond his nineteenth-century grasp and are beyond the scope of this book to explore in technical detail. What Darwin needed was the theory of biological heredity pioneered, unknown to him, by Austrian monk Gregor Mendel (1822-1884), the father of modern genetics. Principles of Mendelian genetics were worked out in the 1860s, discovered by scientists in 1900, and incorporated into the **synthetic theory of evolution** in the 1930s. Until then, in biological circles the theory of evolution by natural selection remained theoretically weak. In anthropology, however, the shadow of Darwinism loomed strong, as it conjured up much of what twentieth-century theoreticians sought to reject.

synthetic theory of evolution

Note

1   For the felicitous phrases "dialogue with the ancestors" and "one dead guy a week," we are indebted to William Fowler and Julia Harrison respectively.

chapter two: the early twentieth century

Twentieth-century anthropological theory represents a sharp break from the nineteenth century. Under the influence of strong anthropological figures, modern American, British, and French national anthropological traditions emerged. In each tradition, anthropologists sought to distance themselves from the unilineal evolutionary and hereditarian doctrines of their predecessors.

American Anthropology

Franz Boas

Almost singlehandedly, Franz Boas (1858-1942) launched American anthropology on the course it maintained throughout most of the twentieth century.

Boas was born and educated in Germany, where he earned a doctoral degree in physics based on research into the optical properties of colour. He took a field trip to northern Canada to study native peoples' perception of colour, and while there became converted to geography and then anthropology. Boas next visited the United States, where he spent time in New York City before becoming a curator at the new Field Museum of Natural History in Chicago. At the Field Museum, he built up an impressive collection of artifacts from the Pacific Northwest Coast, where he did ethnographic and linguistic field research among the Kwakiutl and related aboriginal groups. In the aftermath of a dispute with museum administrators,

Boas left Chicago and joined the faculty of Clark University in Worcester, Massachusetts. A short time later, he moved back to New York and joined the faculty of Columbia University, where he remained for almost half a century.

As Marvin Harris demonstrates in detail in *The Rise of Anthropological Theory* (1968), Boas was principally a cultural anthropologist, but he also did important work in linguistic anthropology, physical anthropology, and, to a limited extent, archaeological anthropology. He was an extraordinarily self-disciplined and prolific scholar, publishing more than 700 articles and books. He also had a strong hand in establishing and strengthening professional organizations like the American Anthropological Association and its flagship journal *American Anthropologist*. The list of anthropologists trained by Boas really does read like a *Who's Who*. For examples, in general anthropology and ethnography, there was Melville Herskovits, E. Adamson Hoebel, Alfred Louis Kroeber, and Robert Lowie; in psychological anthropology, Ruth Benedict and Margaret Mead; in American Indian studies, Alexander Goldenweiser, Paul Radin, and Clark Wissler; and in anthropological linguistics, Edward Sapir. When these students established other anthropology departments — Herskovits at Northwestern University, Sapir at the University of Chicago, and Kroeber and Lowie at the University of California at Berkeley — the Boasian approach to anthropology spread.

In spite of all this personal influence, it is sometimes said that Boas established no anthropological "school." This is because Boas did not make formulating new theory a high priority; rather, he spent much time criticizing old theory from the nineteenth century. Nevertheless, his approach to anthropology had pronounced characteristics. First and foremost, Boas was an ardent empiricist, much more rigorous than his predecessors. He was motivated to record as much information as possible about aboriginal North American Indian cultures being "lost" through assimilation to expanding Euro-American cul-

salvage ethnography tures. This missionary-like zeal for salvage ethnography inspired students and attracted them to anthropology. Furthermore, Boas was an arch-inductivist, urging anthropologists to "let the facts speak for themselves," reject deductive schemes, and avoid premature generalizations. He was particularly critical of the comparative method of classical cultural evolutionists, which made unwarranted use of present-day ethnographic information in reconstructions of the past. Nobody, Boas protested, was "living in the Stone Age." Because he considered evolutionary explanations "one-sided," he urged anthropologists to consider diffusion as another cause of culture change. Overall, Boas wanted detailed, well-rounded stories of cultural development. His approach to anthropology is called **historical particularism,** "historical" because Boas described the present in terms of the past and "particular" because Boas considered the history of each culture to be unique.

historical particularism

Boas was heir to the tradition of Enlightenment egalitarianism, eclipsed during the nineteenth century by a surge of national chauvinism, hereditarianism, and racist views. Racism was particularly strong in nineteenth-century American anthropology, where Samuel George Morton (1799-1851), Josiah Clark Nott (1804-1873), and other members of the "American School" espoused racial polygenism, the doctrine that races are immutable, separately created species. The American School linked polygenism to the defense of black slavery in the ante-bellum American South. Boas insisted that environment dominates heredity in the determination of cultural differences. Having suffered prejudice as a Jew growing up in Christian surroundings, he was determined to shape anthropology into the academic discipline that would demonstrate to the world how race, language, and culture are causally unlinked. He did this creatively with a physical anthropological study of head shape. In nineteenth-century anthropology, head shape — in particular, **cephalic index,** the ratio of head width to head breadth — was considered "fixed" and, because the head contains the brain, a fixed measure of intelligence. Using sophisticated statistical techniques and a large body of data, Boas demonstrated how head shape had changed in only one generation, as the American-born children of immigrants

cephalic index

benefitted from improved health and nutrition and other culturally-conditioned inputs. This landmark study was an important beginning of the attempt to end racism in modern anthropology.

Having come to anthropology from physics, the rigorous Boas might have been expected to model anthropology on natural science. This was not the case. In Germany, he had been influenced by Wilhelm Dilthey (1883-1911) and members of the Neo-Kantian **Southwest School** of German philosophy. This group derived their ideas from philosopher Immanuel Kant (1724-1804), who taught that experience is filtered through innate categories of the mind. Neo-Kantians reformulated Kant's teachings into the proposition that there are two kinds of sciences: *naturwissenschaften*, or natural sciences, and *geisteswissenschaften*, or human sciences of mental phenomena. The natural sciences could aim to be **nomothetic**, or seek explanatory generalizations and laws. The human sciences, however, had to concern themselves with mental phenomena, the core of human existence, and, according to Neo-Kantians, could aim to be only **idiographic**, or seek descriptions of particular events. When Boas converted from physics to anthropology, he had this distinction between generalizing and particularizing sciences in mind. As a result, he stressed culture as a mental construct, paving the way for psychological anthropology and later brands of American anthropology that represented culture as something carried around in people's heads.

Robert Lowie and Alfred Louis Kroeber

The first two anthropologists to earn doctoral degrees under Boas at Columbia were Robert Lowie and Alfred Louis Kroeber.

Robert Lowie (1883-1957) started out with an interest in language and science but, after meeting Boas in New York, switched his interest to anthropology, earning a doctoral degree in 1907 on the basis of fieldwork among American Indians. In 1917, he joined the faculty of the University of California at Berkeley, remaining there until his retirement in 1950. Lowie's first important book was *Primitive Society* (1920), in which he criticized the cultural evolutionary approach,

(margin notes)
Southwest School

naturwissenschaften

geisteswissenschaften

nomothetic

idiographic

especially of Lewis Henry Morgan. Following Boas, Lowie rejected the "one-sided" explanations of cultural evolutionists, although he also rejected extreme versions of diffusionism. There was, he insisted, no *one* determinant of culture. In *History of Ethnological Theory* (1937), Lowie pursued this same line, cautioning anthropologists against theoretical extremism of any kind. Behind his position were intellectual influences shared with Boas, namely the Southwest School of German philosophy and an uncompromising empiricism, in Lowie's case derived from philosopher Ernst Mach (1838-1916). The Lowie program for anthropology consisted of undoing the ethnographic analyses of cultural evolutionists and redoing them in the framework of Boasian historical particularism.

Alfred Louis Kroeber's (1876-1960) first love was literature, but this too changed when he met Boas and decided to take his doctorate in anthropology at the turn of the century. Reflecting his literary background, Kroeber's dissertation was a study of patterns, or configurations, of American Indian style. In 1901, Kroeber moved to California to become curator of the Academy of Sciences Museum. He soon joined the University of California at Berkeley, where he stayed until his retirement in 1946. Kroeber is well known for his textbook *Anthropology* (1923), his ethnographic compendium *Handbook of the Indians of California* (1925), and his theoretical treatise *Configurations of Culture Growth* (1944). While Lowie remained true to Boasian anthropology, Kroeber departed from Boas in an unexpected way. This happened when he promoted the concept of the **super-** **organic**. superorganic

The concept of the superorganic goes back to Herbert Spencer and, after Kroeber, was "revisited" by anthropologist Leslie White. It represents a strong statement of the importance of environment over heredity, "nurture" over "nature" or culture over biology. It also represents an effort to give social scientific disciplines like anthropology a strong identity by showing that they have something special to study — culture, a realm *sui generis*, or unto itself, separate from psychology and "above" biology. Kroeber first published his ideas about the superorganic in 1917 in an article in *American Anthropologist*. In this article,

he stressed the power of culture to shape human behaviour, arguing
against the **great man theory of history**, which stressed the power of
individuals. Using historical examples, Kroeber sought to show that
great men were only great because they happened to be in the right
place at the right time.

great man theory of history

Instead of proposing cultural laws that determine behaviour,
Kroeber proposed cultural patterns or trends. To illustrate the power
of trends, he chose fashion, commonly considered to be subject to
artistic whim and the caprice of the fashion industry. Instead, he
counterargued, fashion features as seemingly capricious as hem
length, lapel shape, and the number and placement of buttons all
change cyclically, precisely enough to be plotted on graphs. The
implication was that while people might *think* they are creative
geniuses or manipulators, in fact they are creatures of culture, imple-
menting changes for which the cultural time is ripe. The superorganic is one example — some say a caricature — of a scientific contrasted with a humanistic orientation for anthropology. It was an unexpected orientation for Kroeber, a student of literature, and especially
since he was a student of Boas, who opposed one-sided explanations.

Throughout his career, Kroeber vacillated back and forth between
the superorganic and traditional Boasian approaches. In 1944, he published *Configurations of Culture Growth*, a book on which he had been
working almost day and night for years. This book was a survey of
major world civilizations, in which Kroeber tried to determine
whether there were any overall trends, or trajectories, of civilized
development. His finding was largely negative: each civilization
appeared to have its own unique trajectory — a historical twist to the
Boasian doctrine of cultural relativism. After *Configurations*, Kroeber
gradually retreated from the concept of the superorganic and
returned to the Boasian fold. Meanwhile, the search for cultural patterns, sometimes called **configurationalism**, had taken a turn into psychological anthropology.

configurationalism

Margaret Mead and Ruth Benedict

Psychological anthropology is a uniquely American contribution to anthropological theory. This school was rooted in the Boasian teaching that culture is a mental phenomenon, popularized by Boas' most famous students, Margaret Mead and Ruth Benedict, and taken in new directions by anthropologists reacting to the psychology of Sigmund Freud.

psychological anthropology

Early psychological anthropologists were curious about the relationship between culture and personality, namely how individuals contribute to culture and how, through enculturation, culture contributes to, or shapes, individuals. Psychological anthropologists understood that this relationship would differ from culture to culture. Under the influence of Boas, they began to incorporate observations of human feelings, attitudes, and other psychological states into their fieldwork and publications. Anthropology became livelier and more engaging as it put on a human face.

enculturation

The anthropologist primarily responsible for this transformation was Margaret Mead (1901-1978). The precocious daughter of academically-oriented parents, Mead grew up in and around Philadelphia, attended college for one year in the American Midwest, and then headed east for what she expected would be a more cosmopolitan education at Barnard College, affiliated with Columbia University. An aspiring poet and writer, she gave up literature when she decided that she lacked the talent for commercial success, and gravitated instead to Boas and his colleague Ruth Benedict, who convinced her that anthropology "mattered." Boas was deeply involved with his effort to use anthropology to counteract hereditarian doctrines, one of which was Freudian psychology, which was then growing in academic popularity. Freud had pronounced that certain phases of human psychological development were fixed by nature and were universal. Boas disagreed, believing that Freud's doctrine was culture-bound, or ethnocentric. He directed Mead to select a psychological phase of individual development, study it in a non-Western culture, and hopefully demonstrate that its manifestation there was different than in the

West. Mead selected, or ended up with, female adolescence in Samoa, a group of islands in the South Pacific. She lived there for several months with the family of a missionary, venturing out into villages to interview a select number of adolescent Samoan girls. The result of this pioneering fieldwork was the first of Mead's many books, *Coming of Age in Samoa* (1928), an all-time anthropology "classic."

The message of *Coming of Age in Samoa* was that female adolescence in Samoa was a psychologically untroubled transition from girlhood to womanhood, during which time Samoan adolescents were spared the "normal" trials and tribulations of sexual awakening because they, unlike their North American counterparts, had been sexually permissive as girls. The conclusion was that adolescence was not troubled by hereditary nature, and the inference was that American adolescents would be less troubled if Americans adopted a more permissive attitude toward sex. Mead's book was an immediate commercial success, garnering public attention because of its bold and controversial pronouncements. The book launched Mead on her life-long career as spokesperson for liberal causes, preaching tolerance and understanding and how learning about exotic behaviour in faraway places provided an opportunity to reflect on "normal" behaviour back home. In this capacity she became the most famous anthropologist of the twentieth century, and the anthropologist primarily responsible for giving anthropology its reputation for cultural relativism.

Mead's other groundbreaking books were *Growing Up in New Guinea* (1930) and *Sex and Temperament in Three Primitive Societies* (1935), which featured ethnographic examples of how sex roles are enculturated and, like adolescence, not programmed by nature. In some of her early work, Mead collaborated with her second husband, Australian anthropologist Reo Fortune, and later she collaborated further with her third husband, British anthropologist and psychological researcher Gregory Bateson. Mead also maintained a close relationship with Ruth Benedict, who encouraged her to persevere and provided counsel in times of distress. In 1982, four years after Mead's death, Australian ethnographer Derek Freeman (b. 1916) published a critical account of her Samoan research in his book *Margaret Mead and Samoa: The Making and Unmaking of an Anthropological Myth.* Freeman took Mead to task (posthumously) for being methodologically superficial and for failing to study Samoan history, which, according to Freeman, involves sexual violence and turmoil that belie Mead's ethnographic portrait of Samoa as a peaceable, sexual paradise. In Freeman's account, Mead is a naive victim of Boas, who pushed her too hard to do research that would turn out the way he wanted. Freeman's book sparked a vigorous, protracted debate among his, and Mead's, defenders and detractors.

When Mead arrived at Columbia, Ruth Benedict (1887-1948) was already there. Benedict had studied literature at Vassar College, taught high school and, like Mead, reluctantly abandoned aspirations to be a commercial poet and writer. Seeking to fill her life with new meaning, she enrolled in an anthropology course at the New School for Social Research in New York City, where she met Franz Boas. Finding anthropology to be an outlet for her creativity, and an intellectual vehicle to explore the underpinnings of her own sense of cultural alienation, she chose anthropology as her career. Benedict did fieldwork under Kroeber, who introduced her to configurationalism, and then returned to Columbia to teach with Boas, helping to train Mead and other distinguished students.

Like Mead, Benedict was interested in the relationship between culture and personality. But while Mead described the culturally conditioned personalities of individuals, Benedict described the personalities of whole cultures. According to Benedict, each culture had its gestalt   own personality configuration, or **gestalt**. Compelling illustrations of this approach were the focus of her book *Patterns of Culture* (1934), for decades a venerated best-seller. In this book, Benedict contrasted the personalities of three cultures: the Kwakiutl of the Pacific Northwest, the Zuñi of the American Southwest, and the Dobuans of the South Pacific. Borrowing names from German philosopher Friedrich Nietzsche (1844-1900), she characterized the Kwakiutl as "Dionysian" because they appeared megalomaniacal and prone to excess, staging vision quests involving self-torture and potlatch ceremonies with conspicuous consumption and destruction of material goods. In contrast, the Zuñi were "Apollonian" because they appeared peaceable and restrained by moderation, with low-key ceremonies that reined in sexual licence. On the basis of ethnographic research conducted by Reo Fortune, Benedict characterized the Dobuans as "paranoid" because they appeared preoccupied with sorcery and suspicious of one another for stealing sweet potatoes. Benedict explained how these three cases illustrated the power of culture to shape divergent normative personalities, resulting in divergent definitions of "deviance." In typical Boasian fashion, she concluded that, because what was deviant in one culture could be normative in another, deviance was not determined by nature.

After *Patterns of Culture*, Benedict continued to implement the Boasian mandate for anthropology by promoting cultural relativism and combatting ethnocentrism and racism both intellectually and politically. To show the concept of race to be scientifically weak and politically destructive, she wrote *Race: Science and Politics* (1945), and during the Second World War she joined other anthropologists in helping to defeat Nazism and the Axis powers by working for the American federal government in Washington, D.C. A result of this morally patriotic effort was her book *The Chrysanthemum and the Sword* (1946), a study of Japanese **national character**. During the Second World War era, other national character studies — sometimes called **culture-at-a-distance** because they had to be done without the benefit of fieldwork — lost anthropological credibility when anthropologists made grandiose generalizations about the ability of childhood personality to shape the cultural behaviour of adults. An infamous case in point was Geoffrey Gorer, who attributed the "obsessive-compulsive" culture of Japan to premature toilet-training, and the "manic-depressive" culture of Russia to prolonged infant swaddling. These theoretical debasements of the psychological approach were caused, in part, by reckless application of the psychology of Sigmund Freud.

national character

culture-at-a-distance

Psychological anthropologists like Mead and Benedict knew about Freudian psychology but were unwilling to use it as the basis of their work. Nevertheless, Boasian-era anthropologists found elements of Freudian theory appealing. Psychological anthropology entered a new phase when anthropologists critiqued Freudian theory, rejected much of it, and then incorporated some of it into a revised theoretical perspective.

The Influence of Sigmund Freud

Sigmund Freud (1858-1939) was a clinical psychologist who tried to help his patients overcome psychological disorders. He became an anthropologist of a sort when he speculated on the origin of these disorders. Ironically, psychological anthropologists rejected most of Freud's anthropological speculations, yet accepted many of his clinical insights.

Freud was born in Vienna into a middle-class family headed by a strict father. In the 1880s, while he was a medical student, he became interested in radical medical experiments in which **hysteria**, a psychological state characterized by morbid or senseless emotionalism, appeared to be cured by hypnosis. Under hypnosis, hysterical patients recalled some experience, usually from childhood, that had been traumatic, then woke up and were no longer hysterical. For Freud, these experiments pointed to the existence of a mental **subconscious**. Patients with psychological disorders had concealed from themselves some action or thought that conflicted with the moral codes of society, Freud thought, and had then repressed the conflict in their subconscious mind, where it festered. Freud set out to determine how such patients might resolve their conflicts therapeutically. He began by studying dreams. In classical Freudian psychology, dreams are expressions of the subconscious mind. They express, in symbolic form, wishes or desires of which society disapproves. Freud probed the subconscious by deciphering dream symbols, most of which were sexual, because Freud believed that sex was the desire that society disapproved of most strongly and therefore the desire most likely to lead to conflict and repression. In 1900, he published these views in his first major book, *The Interpretation of Dreams*.

Freud proceeded to analyze art, literature, religion, and even politics in the same manner he analyzed dreams. These were ideologies and institutions that expressed, in symbolic form, feelings that could not be expressed in reality. They too held clues to repressed desires. Eventually, Freud's distinction between psychologically "sick" and healthy people blurred, and he decided that the subconscious mind was universal. He divided the subconscious, sometimes called the **psyche**, into three levels: the **id**, or libido, the source of desire; the **ego**, or "I," which experienced the outside world; and the **superego**, or conscience, which monitored the id and mediated between the ego and social norms. According to Freud, the ego and superego could be

Margin terms: hysteria, subconscious, psyche, id, ego, superego

moulded by culture, which restrained the id, the animalistic part of human nature with instinctive appetites and drives. The thrust of Freudian psychotherapy was to probe the subconscious to find the source of repressed conflict, make the patient consciously aware of the conflict, and thereby open the door to curing the patient with therapeutic devices.

The Freudian depiction of human nature was pessimistic: everyone was born into a psychological minefield of potential conflict. Some people negotiated this minefield better than others, avoided conflict, and grew up psychologically healthy. Others, less fortunate, succumbed to conflict, developed psychological disorders, and ended up in therapy. After Freud had finished creating his clinical framework, he wondered why this troubled state of human affairs had come into existence. His answer to this question was anthropological, with a Freudian twist.

Freud presented his version of anthropology in a trilogy of three books: *Totem and Taboo* (1918), *The Future of an Illusion* (1928), and *Civilization and its Discontents* (1930). His central insight was that people in the present experience conflict because humanity in the past experienced conflict. Each person relives, or recapitulates, this past as **racial memory**. Freud's account begins with the **pleasure principle**, his name for the natural, libidinous tendency of people to seek psychosexual pleasure and avoid psychosexual pain. Culture opposes the pleasure principle because the consequence of everybody seeking pleasure would be chaos. Most people come to accept that they cannot seek pleasure directly, even though their desire to do so remains a source of tension. Instead, they re-channel, or **sublimate**, their desires into fantasies and institutions which, according to Freud, represent an escape from libidinous reality. These people are acting on the **reality principle**, because they are psychologically mature and realize that acting on the pleasure principle will get them into trouble. Psychologically immature people are inclined to act on libidinous impulse, experience conflict, undergo repression, and became neurotic or psychotic. For Freud, the least "civilized" cultures were the least repressive, so "primitive" adults were like civilized children.

racial memory

pleasure principle

sublimate

reality principle

For Freud, civilization was opposed to human biological nature because civilization tried to tame the animal instincts of people. In fact, civilization was built on sublimated desire. How did this happen? Freud responded with a story about human evolution. The story began with the **primeval family**, which, for Freud, was monogamous, nuclear, and patriarchal, and characterized by unrestricted sex. This family was fraught with problems and could not continue in its original form for very long. In the primeval family, sons desired their mother sexually, but their authoritarian father had priority of sexual access. Therefore, the sons resented their father, even though they respected and loved him at the same time. These ambivalent feelings were a source of major conflict. Eventually, resentment built up to the point where the sons got together and killed their father in the **primal patricide**, an act of profound consequence.

Patricide was a libidinous act that the larger social group recognized as too disruptive to be allowed to recur. Moreover, the sons felt crippling remorse and guilt as a result of what they had done. To prevent a repeat performance, the group created cultural prohibitions — **taboos** — against unsanctioned killing and, equally important, against **incest** that might allow disruptive sexual feelings to come to the fore. The group also invented **totems**, objects of collective veneration, in the form of **father figures**, toward which sons could sublimate their ambivalent feelings. For Freud, these actions ushered in the totemic phase of human history, accompanied by the superego, which insured that the expression of libidinous drives was repressed by guilt.

For men, the psychological legacy of all this was the **Oedipus complex**, named after the legendary Greek son of Laius who unwittingly slew his father and went on to marry his mother. This complex was characterized by unresolved, guilt-inducing desire of men for sexual gratification through their mothers. The corresponding legacy for women was the **Electra complex**, named after the legendary Greek daughter of Agamemnon who sought to kill her mother to avenge her father's murder. The Oedipus and Electra complexes were not equivalent, because Freud believed that male and female sexuality differed fundamentally. From the perspective of late twentieth-century feminism, Freudian theory certainly appears "sexist." A more pertinent observation to be made here, however, is that Freud's account of how each person relives the psychic development of humanity appears to be nineteenth-century cultural evolutionary anthropology in caricature.

Development of Psychological Anthropology

In many ways Freudian theory represented the very kind of anthropology that Boas and his students were trying to overcome. Freud's ideas were highly speculative, overly generalized, evolutionary, hereditarian, sexist, and, in equating non-Western adults with Western children, racist and ethnocentric. We have already seen how Boas used Margaret Mead to try to disprove Freud's pronouncement that adolescent psychosexual turmoil was universal. British social anthropologist Bronislaw Malinowski had a similar goal in mind when he demonstrated that the Oedipus complex was irrelevant for the matrilineal South Pacific Trobriand Islanders, because, in their kinship system, "mother's brother," not "father," was the source of authority over sons. This kind of research showed that if any parts of Freudian theory were to be salvaged for anthropology, the whole theoretical edifice would have to be reconstructed with cross-cultural **variables**.   variables

While finding Freudian theory objectionable and anachronistic, Boasian anthropologists at the same time found it stimulating and engaging. Like anthropology, Freudian psychology was iconoclastic, forcing people to analyze thoughts and behaviour they usually accepted as "normal." And it was a body of thought about personality, a subject in which anthropology could claim no special expertise. Psychological anthropologists were drawn to Freudian psychology in the 1930s and, when this happened, they had to change it in major ways. They abandoned Freud's explanation of psychic evolution, downplayed his emphasis on sex, recast his formulations in terms of cultural relativism, and focused on the development of normal, as opposed to pathological, personality. The result was a new, Freudian phase in psychological anthropology. This phase was characterized by

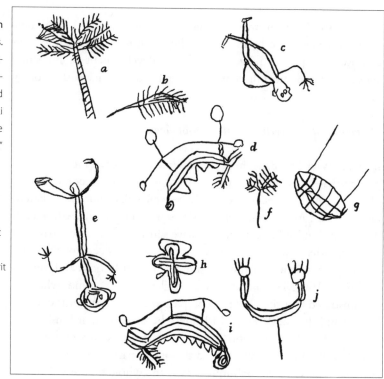

Alorese Youth Drawings.
Cora Du Bois (1903-1991) used these drawings by 14-year old male Atamau Maugliki to interpret Alorese "basic personality."

a. coconut tree
b. fern
c. evil spirit
d. village guardian spirit carving
e. seer's evil familiar spirit
f. fern
g. spirit altar
h. hawk (flower)
i. village guardian spirit carving
j. spirit boat carving

the study of the development of personality cross-culturally, with a strong emphasis on the importance of early childhood experiences.

Freudian anthropology

The chief theoretical architect of **Freudian anthropology** was Abram Kardiner (1891-1981), a psychoanalyst who studied with Freud but who realized that Freud's ideas were culture-bound — a partial product of Freud's own childhood — and had to be overhauled. To accomplish this task, in the late 1930s he convened a seminar of anthropologists in New York City. Major participants included Boasians Ruth Benedict, Ruth Bunzel, Edward Sapir, and Cora Du Bois. Their objective was to develop a theoretical framework for investigating how different cultural experiences nurtured different personality types. With input from the seminar, Kardiner devised a

primary cultural institutions

research model with three major components: **primary cultural**

institutions, secondary cultural institutions, and **basic personality structure.** secondary cultural institutions
Primary institutions were institutions that affected childrearing prac-
tices, for example arrangements for the feeding, weaning, and daily basic personality structure
care of infants. Secondary institutions were the major institutions of
society, politics, and religion. In Kardiner's model, basic personality
structure was shaped by primary institutions and then "projected"
onto secondary institutions, which functioned to help people cope
with the world by depicting the world in familiar, culturally adaptive
terms. Kardiner called this approach **psychodynamic.** psychodynamic

The task of psychodynamic research was to assess primary institutions, secondary institutions, and basic personality structure independently, and then to correlate them in terms of Kardiner's model. To
assess basic personality structure, psychodynamic anthropologists used
clinical tests like the Thematic Apperception Test, or TAT, and the
Rorschach, or "ink blot," test to get informants to "project" their personalities on paper. The first systematic research of this kind was done
by Cora Du Bois (1903-1991) on the island of Alor in the Dutch East
Indies. Du Bois collected Rorschach profiles, children's drawings, and
psychological life histories, which were then sent back for assessment
to clinical specialists in New York. These specialists concluded that the
basic Alorese personality was shallow, indifferent, and apathetic. How
did such a basic personality develop? According to Du Bois, it developed from the early childhood experience of maternal neglect,
caused by Alorese mothers' need to spend extended periods of time
away from their children tending crops in fields. This neglect taught
children to expect that their emotional needs would not be readily
satisfied, with the further consequence that low expectations were
projected onto Alorese religion, characterized by unresponsive deities
and carelessly manufactured effigies. Shaped through this kind of pro-
jection, Alorese religion was able to help children adapt to the maternal neglect they received. Du Bois's book *The People of Alor* (1944) was
the theoretical highpoint of psychodynamic anthropology.

The theoretical lowpoints of psychodynamic anthropology were
the national character studies of the Second World War era, notably
Geoffrey Gorer's studies of Japan and Russia mentioned earlier, which

marked the end of the serious blend of anthropology and Freudian theory. Beginning in the 1950s, innovations in social scientific research methods, in particular the increased use of statistics, prompted anthropologists to distance themselves from Freudian psychology, which, from the perspective of empirical science, appeared rife with ill-defined and un-investigatable concepts. A new generation of psychological anthropologists began to purge anthropology of these concepts and use statistics to make cross-cultural generalizations precise. The pioneering effort in this new direction was John Whiting and Irvin Child's *Child Training and Personality: A Cross-Cultural Study* (1953). Whiting and Child generated cross-cultural data from, among other sources, the new Human Relations Area Files at Yale University and manipulated these data statistically to reveal significant cross-cultural associations. One statistically significant cross-cultural association, described by Marvin Harris in *The Rise of Anthropological Theory*, involved the following traits: prolonged periods of nursing at mother's breast; prolonged post-partum prohibitions of sexual intercourse; polygyny, or the practice of a man having more than one wife; infants sleeping exclusively with their mothers; patrilineality and patrilocality, or determination of genealogical descent and post-marital residence through the male line; and strong, often severe, male puberty rites. In statistics, association does not necessarily imply cause, but statistical association can suggest cause and help narrow the search for cause-and-effect relationships. Anthropologists have been able to link Whiting and Child's traits in a cause-and-effect chain of events beginning with the need for prolonged periods of nursing to supplement dietary protein, and ending with the need for strong male puberty rites to sever the close attachment of son to mother in cultures with male domination. Whiting and Child modified Kardiner's psychodynamic model and renamed its major components. In their model, Kardiner's primary institutions became **maintenance systems**, especially as they affected child training practices; secondary institutions became **projective systems**; and basic personality structure became **personality variables**.

maintenance systems

projective systems

personality variables

In the 25 years between *Coming of Age in Samoa* and *Child-Training and Personality: A Cross-Cultural Study*, American psychological anthropology evolved through pre-Freudian, Freudian, and post-Freudian phases. A brand of anthropology that began as a humanistic, almost literary attempt to make Americans more tolerant of culture and personality differences ended up, in the middle of the twentieth century, following the lead of psychologically "detached" social science.

The Influence of Émile Durkheim

While Franz Boas and his students were promulgating their brands of anthropology in North America, other theoretical influences were at work in France and Britain. In France, classical cultural evolutionism never really took hold. Therefore, when French anthropology assumed its twentieth-century identity, it did not have to reject its nineteenth-century legacy. To the contrary, the theoretical foundation of twentieth-century French anthropology can be found in the nineteenth-century French sociologist Émile Durkheim (1858-1917). Durkheim was also a major influence on key British anthropologists of the early twentieth century, in particular Alfred Reginald Radcliffe-Brown and his theory of structuralism and functionalism. For this reason, Durkheim can be considered a forerunner of the two European schools known as **French structural anthropology** and **British social anthropology**.

French structural anthropology

British social anthropology

Durkheim's theories developed in progression with the publication of four books: *Division of Labour in Society* (1893), *The Rules of Sociological Method* (1895), *Suicide* (1897), and *The Elementary Forms of the Religious Life* (1912). Each book added an ingredient to the recipes for the French and British schools.

In *Division of Labour in Society,* Durkheim explored the diversification and integration of culture, identifying two integrative patterns: older, more "primitive" cultures were less diversified and had little division of labour; more homogeneous, they cohered because individuals were *similar.* Durkheim called this pattern of integration **mechanical solidarity**. Recent, more "civilized" cultures were more

mechanical solidarity

diversified and had considerable division of labour; more heteroge-
nous, they cohered because individuals were *different*. His vision was
of individuals functioning independently, but in harmony — much as
do the various organs of the body to maintain an organism's life.
Because this metaphor seemed so apt, Durkheim called this pattern of
organic solidarity · integration **organic solidarity**. Durkheim's central insight was that social
solidarity could be achieved in two different, organizationally oppo-
site ways. His focus on social coherence, rather than change, represents
a preference for what Auguste Comte called social statics, rather than
social dynamics. The Durkheimian vision of society was very different
from the vision of Karl Marx, who saw solidarity as ephemeral and
society riven with class conflict. For Marx, the state would eventually "wither away" and give rise to communism. For Durkheim, the
more organic solidarity increased, the more government was necessary to regulate socially interdependent parts. Increased organic solidarity submerged the individual in an expanded social reality, as social
interactions superseded individual interactions as determinants of
social life. The academic discipline that would study social interactions
was sociology.

Durkheim established the theoretical framework for sociology in
The Rules of Sociological Method. Social interactions were to be consid-
social facts · ered **social facts** and explained in terms of other social facts, not in
terms of biology or psychology. Behind this pronouncement was
Durkheim's understanding that society was a realm unto itself, *sui
generis*, something like Alfred Louis Kroeber's concept of the superor-
collective · ganic. But Durkheim gave *his* conception of the social realm a special
representations · French twist. For him, social facts were **collective representations** of the
collective consciousness, or **group mind**. This conception was Cartesian,
collective · following the rationalist French philosopher René Descartes, rather
consciousness · than Lockean, following the empiricist British philosopher John
group mind · Locke. Rationalism was a fundamental part of the Durkheimian legacy to French structural anthropology.

In *Suicide,* Durkheim demonstrated how to use his sociological
rules to explain a particular social fact. He chose the fact of suicide,
because suicide was an act that seemed so individualistic yet,

explained sociologically, could be shown to have a strong social dimension. Durkheim correlated types of suicide with patterns of social integration. With mechanical solidarity there was "altruistic" suicide, whereby individuals dissolved themselves into the homogeneous group, while with organic solidarity there was "egoistic" suicide, whereby individuals engaged in a dramatic form of self-expression. When social solidarity was in flux, that is, neither mechanical nor organic, individuals could commit a third type of suicide, brought about by *anomie*, Durkheim's name for the sense of alienation caused *anomie* by the absence of familiar social norms.

The purpose of Durkheim's fourth book, *The Elementary Forms of the Religious Life*, was to expose the societal origins of religion. To Durkheim, "origins" meant something very different than it meant to cultural evolutionists, historical particularists, and other kinds of anthropologists whose orientation was diachronic, and who considered the origin of something to be its source in the past. For Durkheim, the origin of something was its source in the group mind. Accordingly, the elementary forms of religion were collective repre- elementary forms sentations of the collective consciousness of people, who attached sacred meaning to moral principles and then gave those moral principles a social reality in order to make them persuasive. Empiricists have found Durkheim's logic circular: collective representations demonstrate the existence of the collective consciousness, which is posited to demonstrate the existence of collective representations. But Durkheim was not a consistent empiricist; he was a rationalist who believed that knowledge could be independent of observation. Rationalism was imparted to French structural anthropology when the elementary forms of religion of Durkheim became the elementary structures of kinship of Claude Lévi-Strauss.

For Durkheim, the origin of religion, and ultimately of society itself, lay in the impact of social ritual on individuals. His thesis was that "primitive man" (exemplified in particular by aboriginal societies in Australia) experiences a sense of "effervescence" when interacting with his fellows that can only be accounted for by reference to a greater power existing outside of the individual. Once the ritual has ended, and large clans have broken into smaller bands and dispersed to resume the mundane activities associated with "making a living," individuals long for the cascade of sentiment that they had encountered during these periods of togetherness. Durkheim enshrined this distinction between the everyday and the ritual in his oppositional concepts of the **sacred** and the **profane**. These terms are appropriate, because they convey the forms of activity and emotion that surround the pure and powerful occasions of ritual togetherness, as opposed to those that indicate the routine, the mundane, and the "polluted." In particular, Durkheim took great pains to show how the effervescent sensations born in ritual are embodied in **totems**. These objects are, for Durkheim, powerful representations, or elementary forms, which bring these powerful sentiments to the surface of consciousness, even in the absence of ritual. They are therefore icons par excellence of group integration and solidarity. Perhaps more importantly, they serve to remind primitive societies of the greater reality existing just outside themselves, a reality that only fully makes itself felt during social ritual. It is with some justification, therefore, that anthropologists have equated some people's understanding of God with Durkheim's vision of society, for in *The Elementary Forms of the Religious Life* the concepts of God and society do indeed seem interchangeable.

French Structural Anthropology

The intellectual transition from Durkheim to Claude Lévi-Strauss and French structural anthropology was accomplished by Durkheim's student and nephew Marcel Mauss (1872-1950), who, like his uncle, sought to reduce social facts to **elementary structures**. Mauss' ideas are condensed in his essay *The Gift* (1924). Mauss shifted Durkheim's focus from the mind of the group to the minds of individuals. In his scheme, elementary structures of individual minds precede elementary structures of the group mind, which in turn precede elementary structures of the outside world. Mauss was particularly interested in elementary structures of the practice of giving gifts. For him, gift-giving is exchange, or **reciprocity**, which operates according to the elementary principle, "to give, to receive and to repay." Reciprocity is an ingrained mental structure, a logic shared by everyone. Unlike economic anthropologists who consider reciprocity to be restricted to non-market economic transactions, Mauss considered it to be a universal principle of exchange governing, besides economics, social organization and kinship. This was the idea elaborated upon by Lévi-Strauss.

Claude Lévi-Strauss (b.1908) is the guru of French structural anthropology and one of the most celebrated, even if not always understood, anthropologists of the twentieth century. During his years as a student, Lévi-Strauss flirted with politics while immersing himself in the traditions of French ethnography and the ideas of Marcel Mauss. Following fieldwork in Brazil, he turned his attention to anthropological theory, publishing *The Elementary Structures of Kinship* (1949) and *Structural Anthropology* (1958). These books present a complex analysis of kinship based on one aspect of reciprocity: the reciprocal exchange of women.

Working in the tradition of Durkheim, whose concern was solidarity, Lévi-Strauss begins with the proposition that reciprocal exchange among social groups promotes alliances, which facilitate social interaction and make society cohere. These alliances are achieved through the reciprocal exchange of women as "gifts." According to Lévi-Strauss, the propensity, or structure, for gift-giving is innate in the human mind, which operates with a universal logic of dualities, called **binary oppositions**. Lévi-Strauss learned about binary oppositions from the **Prague School** of structural linguists, led by linguist Roman Jakobson (1896-1982), who helped formulate the concept of **phonemes**. In structural linguistics, phonemes are minimally contrasting pairs of sounds that create linguistic meaning. In structural anthropology, binary oppositions are contrasting pairs of mental constructs that create social meaning. Some of the binary oppositions Lévi-Strauss discusses at great length are life versus death, culture versus nature, and self versus other. With binary oppositions, the *relationship* between elements is as important as the elements themselves. This relationship is "mediated." For example, the binary opposition

binary oppositions

Prague School

phonemes

"The Totemic
Operator."
A model of some
"structural" elements of
totemism in the theo-
retical schema of
Claude Lévi-Strauss
(b. 1908).

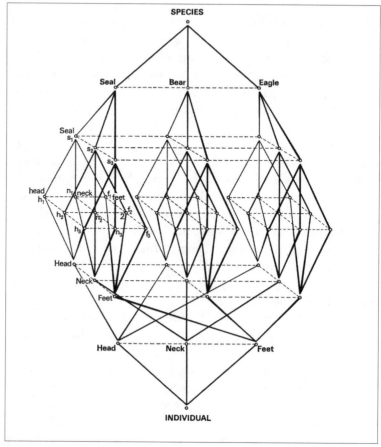

between kinship groups, a transformation of the binary opposition of self versus other, is mediated by the exchange of women. In structuralism, binary oppositions are part of an integrated system of logically connected categories of meaning that structure social activity and the way that activity is conceptualized.

Because Lévi-Strauss analyzes social organization the way structural linguists analyze language, form is as important as content. In the case of the elementary structures of kinship, Lévi-Strauss observes that kinship groups who exchange women create a form, or relationship, among themselves, as well as relationships among exchanged women. This relationship helps to mediate the groups, that is, bring them closer together. Implicated in exchanges of women are four basic relationships: brother and sister; husband and wife; father and son; and mother's brother, or "uncle," and sister's son, or "nephew." Each of these relationships is either "positive," promoting harmony and happiness, or "negative," promoting hostility and antagonism. According to Lévi-Strauss, the mind balances positives and negatives, so in a given exchange system, two of the relationships must be positive and two must be negative. From culture to culture, the content of the relationships can change, but their form, logic or structure remains the same.

In Lévi-Strauss' scheme, the reciprocal exchange of women can assume either of two forms. **Restricted exchange** creates a relationship between two kinship groups through "symmetrical" cross-cousin marriage, whereby brothers and sisters in one group marry cross-cousins — cousins related through parents of the opposite sex — in the other group. **Generalized exchange** creates a relationship between more than two kinship groups through "asymmetrical" cross-cousin marriage, whereby brothers and sisters are not exchanged between two groups directly, but return to their groups after having been circulated through other groups. According to Lévi-Strauss, generalized exchange promotes more solidarity than restricted exchange, because it creates alliances involving more kinship groups. Beyond this, Lévi-Strauss identifies two forms of generalized exchange, one of which he thinks promotes more social solidarity than the other. **Matrilateral cross-cousin marriage**, or marriage to mother's brother's children, leads to a "long cycle" of generalized exchange, while **patrilateral cross-cousin marriage**, or marriage to father's sister's children, leads to only a "short cycle." The long cycle promotes more solidarity than the short cycle, because it creates alliances involving more kinship groups. This difference, Lévi-Strauss thinks, explains why matrilateral cross-cousin marriage is more prevalent than patrilateral cross-cousin marriage in the ethnographic record.

Besides kinship, where Lévi-Strauss has made substantial theoreti-

restricted exchange

generalized exchange

matrilateral cross-cousin marriage

patrilateral cross-cousin marriage

cal contributions to anthropology, structural anthropologists have analyzed a wide range of cultural domains, including, notably, food preferences and myths. In an analysis of the North American Indian myth of the "tricky coyote" (re-analyzed by Marvin Harris in *Cultural Materialism* [1979]), Lévi-Strauss sets up two pairs of analogous binary oppositions, agriculture is to warfare as life is to death, and claims that hunting mediates agriculture and warfare because hunting preserves human life while leading to the death of animals. Scavenging animals like the coyote mediate yet another pair of binary oppositions, herbivore to carnivore, also analogous to life and death, so coyotes must be tricky. In *The Raw and the Cooked* (1969), a book devoted to the structure of cuisine, Lévi-Strauss contrasts raw, cooked, and rotted foods. For cooked foods, boiling is to roasting as culture is to nature. Boiled foods are served to kinspeople while roasted foods are served to strangers, because kinspeople are associated with culture while foreigners are associated with nature. Yet another example of structural analysis is provided by Edmund Leach, who interpreted Levi-Strauss for anglophones. According to Leach, religion is an attempt to bridge the structural opposition between life and death by the creation of the concept of "another world."

One of the most theoretically abstract offshoots of French structural anthropology was structural Marxism. As explained by Marvin Harris in detail in *Cultural Materialism*, under the influence of Lévi-Strauss, structural Marxism developed during the 1970s as an effort to "dematerialize" Marxism, the theory of dialectical materialism, and refocus it on the structure of dialectical thought. Thought, as opposed to behaviour, is implicated by the Marxist concepts of "class consciousness" and "social relations" of the means of economic production. These implications were elaborated by a group of structural Marxists led by Maurice Godelier. Structural Marxism also grew out of an anthropological debate that began during the 1960s between economic **formalists** and economic **substantivists**. Formalists like Scott Cook maintained that the traditional Western definition of economics, the allocation of scarce resources among unlimited wants, also applies to non-Western economies. Substantivists like George Dalton,

formalists
substantivists

Karl Polanyi, and Marshall Sahlins disagreed, maintaining that formalists were ethnocentric and that capitalist conceptions do not apply to economies lacking markets and the political apparatus of states. According to substantivists, people in cultures governed by kinship do not *think* like economic materialists and strategize to maximize their material advantages, because the primary significance of their economic transactions is social. Some substantivists even argued that economic exploitation does not exist if people do not think of themselves as exploited. Pursuing these ideas, structural Marxists like Jonathan Friedman began searching for "hidden" structures, called "dialectical" structures, that make economies tick. Friedman found that the structure of capitalist economies is a fetish for money while the structures of non-capitalist economies are rooted in social and religious values. Meanwhile, in books such as *Islands of History* (1987), Sahlins promoted his notion of "structure" as the *historically* objectified relations of cultural order. The main thrust of structural Marxism has been to transform the theory of dialectical materialism into a theory of dialectical idealism by demonstrating that the structure of economic transactions derives from the structure of thought.

British Social Anthropology

In Britain, the leading early twentieth-century anthropologists were Alfred Reginald Radcliffe-Brown and Bronislaw Malinowski. By force of personality and intellect, these two figures set British anthropology on a theoretical course far different from the course it had followed in the nineteenth century. Working separately and, in the case of Radcliffe-Brown, under the influence of Émile Durkheim, they founded the school known as British social anthropology.

The pivotal "isms" of British social anthropology were **structuralism, functionalism**, and, sometimes, **structural-functionalism**. These "isms" were based on Durkheim's **organismic analogy**, the conceptualization that society is like an organism. Analogies between social and biological phenomena were rooted in the Scientific Revolution, which inspired social scientists to model their enterprise on natural

structuralism
functionalism
structural-functionalism
organismic analogy

Nuer Seasonality.

This is how British social anthropologist E. E. Evans-Pritchard summarized the seasonality of the Nuer of eastern Africa in 1940.

May	June	July	August	September	October	November	December	January	February	March	April

R A I N S   D R O U G H T

R I V E R S   R I S E   R I V E R S   F A L L

H O R T I C U L T U R E   BURNING OF THE BUSH

F I S H I N G

BUILDING & REPAIRING

Preparation of gardens for first millet sowing and for maize

Preparation of gardens for second millet sowing

Harvest maize

Harvest first millet crop

Harvest second millet crop

H U N T I N G A N D C O L L E C T I N G

SCARCITY OF FOOD   P L E N T Y O F F O O D

V I L L A G E S   C A M P S

Older people return to villages

Younger people return to villages

Younger people in early camps

Every one in main dry-season camps

Wedding, initiation, mortuary, and other ceremonies

Main season for raiding Dinka

science, and flourished in the wake of Darwinism, which drew attention to both biological and social evolution. Biological organisms have both structures and functions. The scientific study of organic structure is morphology, while the scientific study of organic function is physiology. According to the organismic analogy, the scientific study of societies should include *social* morphology and *social* physiology. A further inference is that the scientific study of society should include social *evolution*, but British social anthropologists associated evolutionism with nineteenth-century anthropology and did not wish to elaborate this part of the organismic analogy. Their orientation was synchronic, meaning ahistorical, rather than diachronic, or concerned with change through time.

social morphology
social physiology

synchronic
diachronic

The British understanding of "society" was significantly different from the American understanding of "culture." American anthropologists understood culture to comprise economic, social, political, and religious thoughts and behaviour, with both synchronic and diachronic dimensions. In contrast, British anthropologists focused more narrowly on the synchronic study of society. Social structure was the matrix, or enclosing form, of society, while social function was the role that individual parts of society played in maintaining the structural whole. The result of proper social functioning was a social structure maintained in equilibrium or, in terms of the organismic analogy, structural "health." Derived from Durkheimian thought, the twinned theories of structuralism and functionalism inclined British anthropologists to see society as harmonious and stable, unlike evolutionists, who saw culture as prone to change, or Marxists, who saw it as conflicted. British social anthropologists also differed from American historical particularists in their synchronic orientation and their relative lack of involvement with material culture, which American anthropologists maintained through closer affiliations with archaeologists.

social structure
social function

The prototypical British social anthropologist was Alfred Reginald Radcliffe-Brown (1881-1955). Radcliffe-Brown was trained in natural science and inaugurated into anthropology at Cambridge University. While studying at Cambridge, he was influenced by a

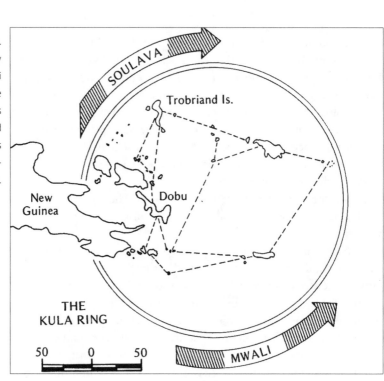

The Kula Ring. As analyzed by Bronislaw Malinowski (1884-1942), in the "ring" necklaces (*soulava*) are exhanged clockwise, armshells (*mwali*) counter-clockwise.

SOULAVA

Trobriand Is.

New Guinea

Dobu

THE KULA RING

50   0   50

MWALI

group of anthropologists who, at the turn of the century, had undertaken an interdisciplinary research expedition to the area of the Torres Strait between Australia and New Guinea. A prominent member of the expeditionary team was William H. R. Rivers (1864-1922), genealogical method founder of the **genealogical method** of anthropology, a method based on the insight that the nub of non-Western social organization is kinship. Radcliffe-Brown did genealogical research among the Andaman Islanders in the Bay of Bengal and made a name for himself with his book *The Andaman Islanders* (1922), a classic ethnography. He held teaching appointments in England, Australia, South Africa, and the United States, where in the early 1930s he taught at the University of Chicago and interacted with Boasian anthropologists like Robert Lowie. Besides *The Andaman Islanders*, his major publications include *African Systems of Kinship and Marriage* (1950), edited with C. Daryll

Forde, *Structure and Function in Primitive Society* (1952), and *A Natural Science of Society* (1948).

Because Britain was a colonial power, British social anthropologists did much of their fieldwork in colonial jurisdictions, notably in Africa. In 1940, British social anthropologists Meyer Fortes (1902-1973) and E. E. Evans-Pritchard (1906-1983) published *African Political Systems*, a controversial book of essays on African ethnography. Some of these essays aimed to counter the contention of evolutionary anthropologists that the evolution of pristine political organization, contrasted with kinship organization, was linked to high population density. The authors cited examples from African ethnography to show that, contrary to this linkage, some groups with low population density had political organization while other groups with high population density lacked political organization. Anthropologists critical of British social anthropology have used *African Political Systems* to illustrate the shortcomings of this approach, which, they argue, paid insufficient attention to African history and therefore failed to recognize that these ethnographic exceptions were evolutionary distortions caused by colonialism and slavery. British social anthropologists have also been criticized for implicitly and explicitly supporting the British foreign policy of indirect rule, which relied on ethnographic knowl- **indirect rule** edge to manipulate, co-opt, and cooperate with native leaders and avoid the need to govern by deployment of brute force.

A second generation of British social anthropologists followed in Radcliffe-Brown's footsteps and broadened his anthropological path. This group included Forde, Fortes, and, notably, Evans-Pritchard, author of the classic ethnography *The Nuer* (1940). Evans-Pritchard moved British social anthropology in a more "cultural" direction by showing how "structures" are not on-the-ground social arrangements per se, but rather "cognitive maps" of these arrangements. Other influential contributors to British social anthropology were Raymond Firth, whose monograph *We, the Tikopia* (1936) added historical and economic dimensions, and Edmund Leach (1910-1989), who in *Political Systems of Highland Burma* (1954) attempted a structural-functional analysis of conflict. American anthropologist Fred Eggan (1906-

1991), a partial convert to structural-functionalism, injected the diachronic perspective of historical particularism. After Radcliffe-Brown, however, the most important British anthropologist of the first half of the twentieth century was Bronislaw Malinowski.

Bronislaw Malinowski (1884-1942) was born and raised in Poland and studied anthropology at the London School of Economics, where he entered the British scene. In 1914, he set out to do fieldwork in New Guinea and had stopped at the Trobriand Islands when the First World War broke out. The British government allowed him to stay in the Trobriands, where he spent several years doing ethnographic research that led to his ethnography *Argonauts of the Western Pacific* (1922), widely regarded as the best of the early classics. Eventually, Malinowski returned to the London School of Economics, where during the 1920s and 1930s he helped train the second generation of British social anthropologists. He also taught briefly at Yale University. The titles of some of Malinowski's books were titillating and "juicy"; for example, *Sex and Repression in Savage Society* (1927) and *The Sexual Life of Savages* (1929). He also wrote *Freedom and Civilization* (1944), *A Scientific Theory of Culture* (1944), and *A Diary in the Strict Sense of the Term* (1967). The diary was published 25 years after Malinowski's death and is noteworthy for its intensely personal, often brooding and melancholy account of his years as a Trobriand fieldworker.

participant-observation   Anthropologists acknowledge Malinowski to be the first and foremost early practitioner of the ethnographic method of **participant-observation**. Using this method, fieldworkers attempt to achieve ethnographic understanding through an artful synthesis of "insider," "subjective" participation and "outsider," "objective" observation. In *Argonauts,* Malinowski also rendered a classic analysis of the Trobriand *kula* ring of economic exchange, and explored Freudian psychology in the context of a non-Western, matrilineal culture. At the level of theory, however, Malinowski's claim to anthropological fame rests primarily on his theory of functionalism.

functionalism   Malinowski's formulation of **functionalism** differed from Radcliffe-Brown's formulation by being rooted in biology *actually* rather than analogously. Like Freud, Malinowski acknowledged that people have basic biological needs, including a basic need for sex. Culture functions to satisfy these basic needs with basic responses. In so doing, it creates a second level of cultural needs, instrumental needs, which are satisfied with instrumental cultural responses. Instrumental responses create integrative cultural needs, which, in turn, are satisfied by integrative cultural responses. This whole theoretical hierarchy of needs and responses that themselves become needs was inspired by Malinowski's fieldwork in the Trobriands, where, according to his own diary, he suffered because his basic biological needs were not being satisfied in a "foreign" culture.

Malinowski and Radcliffe-Brown were antagonists who sparred over theoretical details and never managed to agree on who the *real* functionalist was. Nevertheless, together, like Franz Boas in the United States, they gave British anthropology distinction and a twentieth-century identity.

chapter three: the later twentieth century

Early in the twentieth century, then, we can note that both the British and French schools of social research fell heavily under the sway of Émile Durkheim and his intellectual progeny, especially Mauss, Lévi-Strauss, and Radcliffe-Brown. In North America, meanwhile, an altogether different configuration of anthropological knowledge was taking shape under the careful tutelage of Franz Boas. Unlike the structuralist and functionalist perspectives espoused by the Europeans, American anthropologists cultivated an avowedly historical approach that emphasized the radical diversity of cultural form, rather than its psychosocial solidarity. Despite its emphases on change through time and empiricism, this epistemology of culture historicism often sacrificed breadth of analysis for the sake of precision. As a result, even those innovations made by Mead and Kroeber have been seen by subsequent generations as impoverished theoretically. The perceived central weakness of historical particularism, then, was precisely its inability to grasp with broader, cross-cultural historical patterns and processes.

In the later decades of the twentieth century, this tension between the particular and the general was to emerge as a central problem on both sides of the Atlantic for the newly professionalized discipline of anthropology. While the nineteenth-century evolutionist schemes developed by Morgan and Tylor no longer seemed tenable to the increasingly sophisticated student of culture, the largely descriptive approach championed by Boas also seemed inadequate, in that it suffered from a dearth of explanatory theory. What was needed was a perspective that charted a middle course between these extremes: an approach that united historical change and variation with social structure and integration, all within an analytically powerful body of theory. In addressing this need, the work of several anthropologists, including Leslie White and Julian Steward (who will be discussed in subsequent sections), has been very influential. Among the most enduring and influential of later twentieth-century perspectives for anthropology, particularly in its most recent guises, has been that of German sociologist Max Weber.

The Legacy of Max Weber

Durkheim employed an organic analogy to understand how social groups cohere, and Marx understood control of the material conditions of life to be the engine driving human history. Both theorists therefore believed that forces existing outside the individual (psychosocial on the one hand, dialectical on the other) act to condition cultural meaning and structure social relations. In neither formulation
agency is much room left for the creative **agency** of individuals, and, in fact, both Durkheim and Marx are often criticized for treating the subjects of their theories as homogenous drones, mindlessly obeying the relentless forces that shape and control every facet of their existence.

In contrast, and alone of these three great social theorists of the nineteenth and early twentieth centuries, German Max Weber (1864-1920) is credited with viewing active, thinking individuals as central to the creation, maintenance, and innovation of social and cultural
idealistic forms. For this reason, his work is often thought of as **idealistic** or "ideational," and is frequently contrasted with the materialism of Marx. Such a characterization is misleading, because the creative agency that Weber attributes to individuals — the ideational — is nevertheless grounded in the relations of production and reproduction in any given society. In part because his work has so effectively synthesized the supposedly antithetical forces of idealism and materialism, Weber has been deeply influential in anthropological writing throughout the twentieth century, and has become especially impor-

tant with the rise of **political economy** and **postmodernism** in the 1970s
and 1980s.

In two of his most important works, *The Protestant Ethic and the
Spirit of Capitalism* (1920) and *The Sociology of Religion* (1922), Weber
presented his strategy for understanding how societies develop
through time. Although his ideas were essentially evolutionist, they
bore little resemblance to the unilineal theories of his nineteenth-
century contemporaries Edward Burnett Tylor or Lewis Henry
Morgan. Rather than reducing the great variety of social forms in the
world to a single, unidirectional model that charts social evolutionary
change from the "primitive" through the "civilized," Weber sought a
theory that placed existing beliefs and structures in particular historical contexts. For this reason, he is often thought of as a **multilineal**
evolutionist whose theory accounts for the great diversity of human
life, but resists the temptation to rank this diversity according to a
rigid, **Eurocentric** scale of norms and values.

The principal elements of Weber's schema may be outlined as fol-
lows. Complex societies arise from a progressive differentiation and
intensification of labour, which in turn gives rise to a stratified hierarchy of social and economic classes. As a given social and historical
environment grows in complexity, so too do the material inequities
between these classes. These inequities, notably between the ruling
elite and military classes and what Weber calls the **relatively non-privileged** classes of urban artisan and merchant, lead the latter to experience both a profound sense of alienation from sociopolitical power
and a growing awareness of economic marginalization. This discrep-
ancy between the world of their experience and that of their expec-
tation (what *is*, as opposed to what *should be* — the problem of evil,
or **theodicy**) is embodied in and expressed through an explicitly religious framework.

This point is crucial to Weber's model because, in his view, **religion**
is the engine that drives social transformation through time. The mer-
chant-class's despair and alienation from power foster deep anxieties
about the apparent senselessness of the world: if one lives in accordance with a good and powerful deity's wishes, fulfilling all **ritual**

political economy
postmodernism

multilineal

Eurocentric

relatively non-privileged

theodicy

religion

ritual

observances and prescribed behaviour, why does the world continue to be so problematic? This dilemma cries out, Weber maintains, for resolution. There is a need, using his terminology, for salvation from the world. Coming to the heart of his formulation of social change, Weber believes that this salvation is accomplished through the radical restructuring of beliefs about the world, which in turn prescribes ethical behaviours to bring people into accord with this new vision.

salvation

ethical

Inner-worldly asceticism is the central disposition involved in this process, because it entails "removing" oneself from corrupt worldly indulgences, while (paradoxically) remaining within the world of human activity. For Weber, inner-worldly asceticism opposed the "outer-worldly" ascetics — monks, hermits, etc., — who seek literally to escape the social world and its influences by retreating to special spaces (e.g., monasteries, deserts) where worldly things have no power or authority. By refraining from indulgence in specific corruptions which inhere in the world, the inner-worldly ascetic remains virtuous (by Judeo-Christian standards) even while participating in other, non-corrupting aspects of worldly life. Crucially for Western society, material prosperity is not only excluded from this catalogue of iniquity, but becomes a hallmark of one's standing *vis-à-vis* divine will. The stimulus for such reformulation and renewal is understood to come from especially creative individuals, charismatic prophets, who generally claim to receive a new revelation of divine Truth that will re-integrate belief and action, and in so doing restore psychosocial harmony to humanity.

Inner-worldly

asceticism

charismatic prophets

For Weber, the most significant example of an embodiment of this process occurred in the form of Calvinist Protestantism, an urban merchant's religion that rationalized a new relationship between human beings and God. In this way, John Calvin (1509-1564), the French theologian, is to be considered a prophet, bearing a new vision of human life. Under this new covenant "revealed" to Calvin, individuals are directed to recreate heaven on Earth through hard work, as prescribed by God in Scripture, and obedience to the divine will. Middle-class professionals, namely merchants and artisans, are elevated to a position of ethical superiority in this model;

Calvinist Protestantism

rationalized

no longer are they to be ideologically dominated by ruling elites. Rather, urban merchants and artisans come to view themselves as a community of believers united by certain ethical tenets, adherence to which will certainly lead to a more materially rewarding and emotionally satisfying life. A merchant might therefore look to his material prosperity as a sign of God's grace, or lack thereof. The burgeoning culture of sixteenth-century Renaissance commerce, once linked in this way to a **cosmological order**, became an increasingly compelling blueprint for action in the world. If people behaved in a certain way, in accordance with God's will, they could expect to be materially rewarded in the here and now, and spiritually justified in the hereafter. Small wonder, then, that this new system of meaning and action ultimately resulted in the global triumph of industrial capitalism.

cosmological order

Weber's ideas about social evolution have been especially useful to anthropologists of recent generations, because there has been an increasing reluctance to view societies and cultures as the static, pristine organisms of Durkheimian theory. Moreover, in recent years the discipline has become more concerned with issues pertaining to the creative agency of individuals, the cultural worlds they construct and inhabit, and the various permutations of consensus and conflict that exist within and between cultures. Among those responsible for adapting Weber's thought to explicitly anthropological analysis, one of the most prominent has been Anthony F. C. Wallace. In his influential historical ethnography about the Iroquois, *The Death and Rebirth of the Seneca* (1972), Wallace applies his concept of the **revitalization movement**, which is more fully formulated in his theoretical work *Religion: An Anthropological View* (1966). In both, the author draws heavily on Weber's idea that during periods of cultural dissonance or crisis, it is the charismatic prophet who rationalizes a new and more satisfying religious worldview for the members of a society. A second now-classic Weberian study is Peter Worsley's *The Trumpet Shall Sound* (1968), in which many indigenous peoples of Indonesia and New Guinea are led by a variety of charismatic prophets in a series of millennial "cargo cults." Worsley's and Wallace's studies are strikingly similar in

revitalization movement

that both sociocultural contexts examined are ones in which colonial powers place severe economic, political, and cultural stress on the colonized, generating a "breakdown" in the indigenous social order. In both settings, the revitalizing social movements rationalize the impact of colonialism into worldviews that stipulate the omnipotence of a supernatural power or agent who will ultimately restore harmony and happiness if specific ethical and behavioural criteria are adhered to. More recently, Jean and John Comaroff's *Of Revelation and Revolution* (1991) has analyzed the impact of colonialism in South Africa applying many of the same concepts. In light of these and similar analyses, which highlight the transformative potential of human agency, Weber's synthesis of materialism and idealism has seemed in some ways more useful than Marx' theory, which is often viewed as reducing culture to an effect of material concerns.

Cognitive Anthropology

The full impact of Weber's legacy in anthropology was not really felt until four or five decades after his death. In the meantime, as mid-century anthropology expanded and diversified, especially in North America, a number of new theoretical approaches emerged as continuations of, or reactions to, Boasian historical particularism. One such approach was cognitive anthropology.

Cognitive anthropology   **Cognitive anthropology** was rooted in Boasian cultural relativism with input from anthropological linguistics. Its theoretical orientation emic   was **emic**, contrasted with **etic**. The contrast between emics and etics etic   in anthropology originated in the 1950s with linguist Kenneth Pike, phonemics   who made an analogy with the contrast between **phonemics** and **pho-** phonetics   **netics** in linguistics. Phonemics is the study of linguistic *meaning*, while phonetics is the study of linguistic sounds. Linguistics can study the sound systems of languages by themselves, with language speakers supplying raw data. To discover which sounds are meaningful, however, they must rely on language speakers as authorities. Phonetics represents the point of view of the "outsider," the linguist investigator, while phonemics represents the point of view of the "insider," the

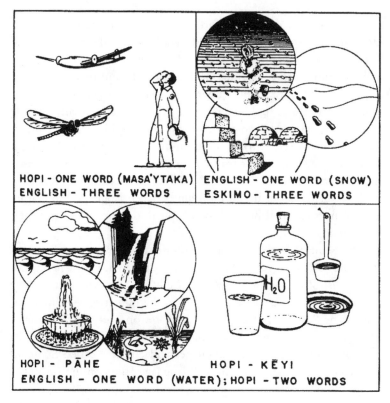

The Sapir-Whorf Hypothesis.
The hypothesis states that languages, in this case Hopi and English, classify experiences differently.

speaker being investigated. Relating this distinction to the anthropological fieldwork technique of participant-observation, Pike decided that participation was "emic," because, in principle, its goal was to enable anthropologists to think and behave like natives, while observation was "etic," because its goal was to have anthropologists remain detached. The emic approach was "seeing things from the native's point of view," which, according to Pike, would promote cross-cultural understanding and combat ethnocentrism in accordance with the doctrine of cultural relativism. Pike advocated both emic and etic approaches to anthropology, but preferred the emic.

Another source of cognitive anthropology was the **Sapir-Whorf hypothesis**, named after anthropological linguistic Edward Sapir and

Sapir-Whorf hypothesis

his associate Benjamin Lee Whorf. Sapir (1884-1939) was a student of Boas and close friend of Benedict and Mead. Like Benedict and Mead, he wrote poetry and explored the relationship between personality and culture. Talented both artistically and mathematically, Sapir devoted most of his career to the study of language, first in Canada, then at the University of Chicago, and finally at Yale University, where he co-founded the anthropology department. Whorf (1897-1941) worked for an insurance company in Hartford, Connecticut, not too far from Yale in New Haven, where he met Sapir. Under Sapir's influence, Whorf disciplined his penchant for philosophizing about the relationship between language and culture and in the 1930s collaborated with Sapir in the formulation of their hypothesis.

The Sapir-Whorf hypothesis expresses the view that the mental structures of languages and cultures are correlated. The structures of languages influence the structures of cultures, and vice versa. Sapir and Whorf were especially interested in the influence — sometimes said to be "determining" — of language on culture. Their chief example was a contrast between the Hopi language and culture and a combination of European languages and cultures called Standard Average European, or SAE. In SAE languages, the concept of time is "objectified" by being quantified in expressions such as "ten days." In contrast, in the Hopi language, time is "subjectified" by lacking quantification in expressions that instead represent time as a process of "becoming later." SAE languages also use objective "mass" nouns like "food" and "water," which must be individualized with adjectives like "some" and adjectival phrases like "a glass of." In contrast, the Hopi language lacks mass nouns; instead, every noun is individualized, rendering it subjective without the need for qualification. Furthermore, SAE speakers objectify the concept of space by using spatial metaphors in rhetorical expressions such as "make a point," "grasp an idea," and "come straight to the conclusion." In contrast, Hopi speakers subjectify space with special parts of speech called "tensors." In each of these cases, according to Sapir and Whorf, the contrast between the structure of SAE and Hopi languages is correlated with a contrast between objectifying SAE and subjectifying Hopi cultures, which "structure" the world differently. Like French structuralists, Sapir and Whorf believed that culture is carried around in people's heads as a classificatory logic that creates meaning. Different cultures have different meaning systems which, like the phonemic systems of language, are equally worthy yet mutually incomprehensible in the absence of a means of cross-cultural communication.

Cognitive anthropology emerged during the 1960s when a faction of American anthropologists, growing out of the tradition of Boas, sought to make their emic orientation explicit and, inspired by linguistics, improve their methodological rigour. The school, sometimes called **ethnoscience**, **ethnolinguistics** or the **New Ethnography**, is best known for its investigative techniques, devised mainly by practitioners Harold Conklin, Charles Frake, and Ward Goodenough. The object of these techniques was to describe native cognition, or perception, as a **semantic domain**, or domain of meaning, with a cognitive "code" that could be "cracked." The most compelling technique of this sort was **componential analysis**, which generated **folk taxonomies** of meaning resembling the Linnaean taxonomy of Western biology. The Linnaean taxonomy is a classification of the realm of living things using a hierarchy of categories defined by biological criteria. Likewise, folk taxonomies were classifications of cultural realms using hierarchies of categories defined by cultural criteria. The goal of componential analysis was to uncover these criteria. By interviewing native informants in the manner of anthropological linguists, who utter contrasting sounds and then ask informants whether the contrasts are meaningful, componential analysts produced "cultural grammars," or "maps" of semantic domains, ranging from Subanum boils and Zeltal firewood to "ethnobotanical" classifications of Amazonian pharmaceutical plants. Cognitive anthropologists shared the view that culture is a formal system of rules for thought and behaviour. Unlike in Western biology, however, where the Linnaean classification is held

ethnoscience

ethnolinguistics

New Ethnography

semantic domain

componential analysis

folk taxonomies

to be "right" and folk classifications of living things "wrong," in cognitive anthropology all classifications were treated as culturally context-dependent.

The popularity of cognitive anthropology peaked in the 1960s and then declined, but not before the school had attracted criticism from anthropologists of opposing theoretical orientations, conspicuous among them new cultural evolutionists and materialists.

Cultural Neo-Evolutionism

By the time Franz Boas died, his grip on American anthropology had loosened. In the post-Boasian era, historical particularism faded into the background of an increasingly crowded picture of anthropological theories. One new element in this picture was a revival of a nomothetic anthropology, which had been eclipsed by Boas' preference for idiographic approaches. The search for cross-cultural generalizations was aided by the Human Relations Area Files, established in the 1940s by George Peter Murdock at Yale University and used in the 1950s to do research for Whiting and Child's *Child Training and* cultural neo- *Personality*. The outstanding new nomothetic theory was **cultural neo-** evolutionism **evolutionism**, a reformulation of nineteenth-century classical cultural evolutionism that in some ways was *anti*-Boasian.

The new cultural evolutionism was the brainchild of four American anthropologists, Leslie White, Julian Steward, Marshall Sahlins, and Elman Service, with input from British archaeologist V. Gordon Childe. The theory originated with White (1900-1975), an anthropologist trained in the Boasian tradition but who broke rank with Boas radically during his long career at the University of Michigan. White's controversial views are summarized in two books, *The Science of Culture* (1949), a collection of essays, and *The Evolution of Culture* (1959), an exposition of the course and process of evolution.

White considered culture to be a system of its own kind, *sui gener-is*, akin to Kroeber's concept of the superorganic. Cultural "laws" culturology would constitute the science of **culturology**. The linchpin of the system was **thermodynamics**, the study of the conversion of forms of energy in the universe. White was impressed with the **second law of thermodynamics**, which stated that the universe is running down structurally and dynamically, resulting in increased **entropy**, or disorder. According to White, biological evolution works in the opposite direction, taking "negative entropy" from the universe and increasing order in the production of complex forms of life. Cultural evolution, which supplants biological evolution in the case of *Homo sapiens* and ancestral species, enhances this trend. To explain the evolution of culture, White proposed a **thermodynamic law**: culture evolves as the amount of energy harnessed per capita per year is increased, or as the efficiency of the means of putting this energy to work is increased. The law was symbolized $E \times T = C$, energy times technology equals culture. White defined four major stages of cultural evolution, each of which began with an energy "revolution." The first revolution was the invention of tools, which increased the ability of the human body to obtain food calories. The second revolution was the "Neolithic Revolution," a term coined by archaeologist Childe to describe the increased control over food energy achieved by the domestication of plants and animals. The third and fourth revolutions were the harnessing of fossil fuels in the eighteenth century and atomic energy in the twentieth century. In between these revolutions, culture evolved as the technology for using these new energy sources improved.

An integral part of White's thermodynamic system was his **layer-cake model of culture**, a depiction of culture comprising three layers, with a layer of technology and economy at the bottom, a layer of ideology at the top, and a layer of social and political organization in the middle. In the "determination" of cultural evolution, the bottom layer predominated, because innovations in technology and energy took place there. In assigning priority to technology and economy over ideology as the impetus for cultural change, White was an avowed cultural materialist. Some of his materialism came from Marxism, which he is alleged to have "discovered" on a trip to the Soviet Union in the 1920s. Connected to Marxism was Lewis Henry Morgan, whose views on the importance of private property

thermodynamics

second law of thermodynamics

entropy

thermodynamic law

layer-cake model of culture

impressed Friedrich Engels. White also "discovered" Morgan and became determined to rehabilitate Morgan's reputation as a cultural evolutionist while criticizing Franz Boas for bringing that reputation into disrepute. White's criticism of Boas (posthumously) was even stronger than Derek Freeman's criticism of Margaret Mead.

While White was promulgating evolutionism in Michigan, an antagonist was gathering strength in Illinois. That antagonist was cultural ecology Julian Steward (1902-1972), the "father" of modern cultural ecology. Steward, another Boasian by intellectual upbringing, was a long-time professor at the University of Illinois, where he helped train a host of distinguished political and economic anthropologists, including Morton Fried, Andrew Vayda, Eric Wolf, and Elman Service. Cultural ecology nurtured a nomothetic approach to anthropology because it focused on the articulation between culture and nature, linking anthropology to nomothetic natural sciences like biology, demography, and chemistry. Steward's work grew out of the "culture area" concept used by Boasians Alfred Louis Kroeber and Clark Wissler to demarcate American Indian groups. Each group inhabited a geo- adaptation graphical area to which, through culture, it adapted. Adaptation became the rubric of cultural ecology.

In 1936, Steward published a seminal essay on the economic and band social basis of bands. In this essay he defined band as distinguished from what Service later called "tribe," "chiefdom," and "state." He also defined three types of bands — patrilineal, matrilineal, and "compos- ite" — and linked each type to particular ecological circumstances. Steward's approach prompted some Boasians to rethink their eclectic approach to anthropological explanation and concentrate instead on cultural ecology. The result was a reinterpretation of some famous anthropological events, notably the Northwest Coast ceremony of potlatch the potlatch, which Ruth Benedict had depicted as a conspicuously wasteful drive for social status but which Helen Codere and Wayne Suttles later explained as an ecologically adaptive redistributive feast.

As a cultural ecologist, Steward was not *primarily* a cultural evolu- tionist. Nevertheless, he took enough interest in evolutionism to find White's pronouncements extreme. Steward distanced himself from

White by calling White's brand of evolutionism **universal** and his own universal
brand **multilineal**. He called the nineteenth-century brand **unilineal**. multilineal
Implied by these labels was Steward's view that he was a specialist unilineal
while White was a generalist. The labels "unilineal" and "multilineal"
meant that classical cultural evolutionists believed that evolution pro-
ceeds in only one direction and cannot skip stages, whereas Steward
believed that evolution can branch off in numerous directions as cultures adapt to varied circumstances. For years, Steward and White
sparred over points of cultural evolutionary theory, with Steward
accusing White of being so general that he could not explain anything in particular and White accusing Steward of being so particular
that he could scarcely be called an evolutionist. It took two colleagues
of Steward's and White's, Sahlins and Service, to resolve this dispute in
1960.

Marshall Sahlins and Elman Service were colleagues at the
University of Michigan, where they worked in close association with
White. As a student of Steward's, Service maintained an interest in the
ecological basis of social groupings, the theoretical framework for his
popular text *Primitive Social Organization* (1962). Sahlins began his
work in economic anthropology and was a strong proponent of cultural evolutionism and materialism before he began to combine
French structural and historical analyses in the late 1960s. In 1960,
Sahlins and Service co-authored *Evolution and Culture*, in which they
sought to reconcile the views of Steward and White. In the time-
honoured anthropological tradition of treating biology and culture as
analogues, Sahlins and Service argued that, like biological evolution,
cultural evolution has two different dimensions. The dimension of
general evolution was being pursued by White, who was concerned
with long-range evolutionary progress and trends, while the dimension of specific evolution was being pursued by Steward, whose
explanation of local adaptation was analogous to Darwin's mechanism of natural selection. Having demonstrated that White and
Steward were really complementary rather than antagonistic, Sahlins
and Service settled down to a decade of work together at Michigan,
where, with White, they formed a powerful evolutionary triumvirate.

The Michigan "school" influenced a number of other cultural evolutionists and ecologists, for example, Alexander Alland, Jr., Robert Carneiro, and Yehudi Cohen, who kept the nomothetic approach to cultural anthropology alive.

functionalist archaeology

The new cultural evolutionism had a major impact on prehistoric archaeology, mainly through White. Since its establishment in the mid-nineteenth century, prehistoric archaeology had progressed through several stages linked to stages in the development of cultural anthropology. There was functionalist archaeology, Marxist archaeology, and, under the influence of Boas, culture-historical archaeology, represented in the United States by the Midwestern Taxonomic Method. Archaeologist Betty Meggers, a student of White, was inspired by White's thermodynamic formula for cultural evolution, $E \times T = C$. Finding the culture-historical approach unproductive, she decided to apply the formula to archaeology, believing that if archaeologists *knew* technology (T) and environment (E), they could *reconstruct* culture (C). This idea was developed further by another student of White's, Lewis Binford, who became the leader of the New Archaeology of the 1960s.

Marxist archaeology

culture-historical archaeology

Midwestern Taxonomic Method

New Archaeology

Binford grew up with the "old," culture-historical archaeology but changed under the influence of White. He decided that archaeology ought to be an integral part of anthropology because archaeologists and anthropologists share the same goal: to explain similarities and differences among cultures. To "explain" means to offer generalizations about cultural systems and cultural evolution. Binford acknowledged that cultures change in response to both the natural environment and other cultures, but he maintained that, in explaining change, some parts of culture are more important than others. He rejected the conception of culture as "shared values," a conception promulgated by psychologically-oriented students of Boas's like Benedict and, later, Clyde Kluckhohn (1905-1960), for whom culture was ethos, or spiritual character. Instead, Binford adopted White's layer-cake model of culture and argued that, in archaeology, artifacts, as objects of material culture, can reflect all three layers, yielding a well-balanced picture of cultures in the past. To realize this potential,

ethos

archaeologists need to be trained as ethnologists, so they can learn how artifacts function in the present and then "read" these functions back in time. Under Binford's influence, the new archaeology revived the nineteenth-century "comparative method."

Aiming to make archaeology scientific, Binford adopted a number of nomothetic devices. One device was the **hypothetico-deductive model** for scientific explanation, developed by philosopher-of-science Carl G. Hempel. This model directed scientists to hypothesize "covering laws," from which specific circumstances could be deduced — predicted or retrodicted — and then compared with empirical reality. Another device was **general systems theory**, a cybernetic model for culture that involved "feedback loops" and "positive," or system-maintaining, and "negative," or system-changing, cause-and-effect chains. Binford argued vigorously against psychological explanations of culture. Like White and (Kroeber when he promoted the concept of the superorganic), Binford opposed the great man theory of history, believing instead that human behaviour is determined by forces — laws — of which individuals are largely unaware and over which they can exert little control.

This hyper-scientific, anti-humanistic, and "positivist" attitude made the new cultural evolutionism and the New Archaeology pills too bitter for many anthropologists to swallow. Because of its preoccupation with cultural process, the New Archaeology came to be called **processual archaeology**. Beginning in the 1980s, processual archaeology attracted severe criticism from **post-processualists**, who saw in it almost everything that was wrong with modern science. At the same time, in cultural anthropology, "postmodernists" severely criticized modern science for many of the same reasons.

Cultural Materialism

An important part of the resurgence of nomothetic anthropology in the post-Boasian era was **cultural materialism**, an unabashedly scientific perspective developed by Marvin Harris (b.1927). The tenets of cultural materialism can be found in three of Harris's many books: *The*

Nature of Cultural Things (1964), *The Rise of Anthropological Theory* (1968), and, especially, *Cultural Materialism* (1979). Harris began to develop cultural materialism in an effort to purge modern anthropology of some of the legacy of Boas and continued to develop it in an effort to combat the spread of new nonscientific and antiscientific attitudes in the profession.

Cultural materialism addresses a central problem for scientific anthropology: people can be both subjects and objects of scientific investigation. People can think and say things about themselves, just as scientists think and say things about them. Where, then, does true knowledge reside? The answer, according to Harris, can be found by maintaining two pairs of cross-cutting epistemological criteria: mental versus behavioural domains and emic versus etic domains. The mental domain is what people *think*, the behavioural domain, what people *do*. As explained in the earlier exposition of cognitive anthropology, the emic domain belongs to the participant, the etic domain to the observer. Combined, these two pairs of distinction yield four epistemological perspectives: the emic behavioural perspective is what people think about their own behaviour; the emic mental perspective, what people think about their own thoughts; the etic behavioural perspective, what the observer observes about other people's behaviour; and the etic mental perspective, what the observer observes about other people's thoughts. While all four perspectives are *possible*, two are *problematic* and ought to be approached with caution. The emic behavioural perspective is problematic because,
false consciousness according to Harris, people can develop **false consciousness** and misrepresent the meaning of their own behaviour to themselves and to others. The etic mental perspective is problematic because it is difficult to find out what is going on inside someone else's head. According to Harris, the etic behavioural and emic mental perspectives lack these drawbacks and are more likely to yield useful information.

In Harris' understanding of scientific anthropology, there is room for both emic and etic perspectives, but they must be kept separate and maintain their own operational definitions and data languages. In the end, the etic perspective predominates. In emics, the native informant is the ultimate judge of validity; in etics, it is the scientific observer. Both natives and scientists can be "objective," but when natives are objective they themselves become scientists. For Harris, objectivity is not mere intersubjectivity, or mutual understanding and the ability to participate in one another's cultures; there is only one objective truth — the etic truth of science.

Like White, Harris divides culture into several levels, which form a universal pattern. Harris' levels are mode of production, mode of reproduction, domestic economy, political economy, and behavioural superstructure. Each has an etic behavioural dimension and an emic mental dimension. Favouring the etic behavioural dimension, Harris combines the modes of production and reproduction into the component *etic behavioural infrastructure*, combines domestic and political economies into the component *etic behavioural structure,* and relabels behavioural superstructure the component *etic behavioural superstructure.* A fourth component, *mental and emic superstructure*, applies to all levels of the universal pattern. The core of cultural materialism is the principle of infrastructural determinism, the name Harris gives to his presupposition that, more often than not, culture changes first in the etic infrastructure and then reverberates through etic structure and superstructure to affect emic superstructure last. In Harris' vocabulary, contrasted with cultural materialists, cultural idealists explain culture change as occurring in the opposite direction, while cultural eclectics explain culture change inconsistently. universal pattern

infrastructural
determinism

idealists

eclectics

The "materialism" in cultural materialism derives from Marxism, which Harris acknowledges as the source of this part of his theory. But, according to Harris, Marx and Engels omitted mode of reproduction from their formulation, confused mental and behavioural and emic and etic realms, and were saddled with the Hegelian dialectic, a metaphysical rather than scientific principle. Once Harris rid dialectical materialism of these "mistakes," the name cultural materialism seemed more appropriate.

Why infrastructural determinism? According to Harris, it is because infrastructure is the primary interface between culture and nature and the place where people are obliged to start using culture to cope with nature in orderly ways. Scientists, looking for order, are probably going to find it there.

As a theoretical agenda for anthropology, cultural materialism has much in common with neo-evolutionism and the New Archaeology. All three of these approaches are, or were, staunchly pro-science. All have been espoused by strong anthropology personalities, who have been criticized for intolerance, "one-sidedness," and a lack of appreciation for alternative, "culturally sensitive" ways of doing anthropology. Nevertheless, these personalities joined forces with many of their critics to condemn another trend in late twentieth-century anthropology: the trend to biologize cultural anthropology.

Biologized Anthropology

Despite differences, the foregoing Boasian and post-Boasian anthropological "isms" shared an opposition to hereditarian interpretations of human cultural variation. "Nurture," versus "nature," was a hallmark of twentieth-century anthropology. In Britain, France, and the United States, modern anthropologists sought to put Darwin's century, the nineteenth century, behind them.

In the decades following the Second World War, from the late 1940s through the early 1970s, anthropology expanded in universities, especially in North America, where the discipline was organized into the four subdisciplines of cultural, biological, archaeological, and linguistic anthropology. As universities prospered, these subdisciplines grew and became highly specialized, but cultural anthropology dominated, attracting by far the largest number of practitioners and setting the intellectual tone for the profession. Meanwhile, in biological anthropology, specialists like osteologists, primatologists, and geneticists practiced their trades largely unbothered and ignored by their more academically influential colleagues. But in the 1960s, this hands-off relationship changed.

The impetus for change was the emergence in biological anthropology of an interest in the biology of human *behaviour*. Preliminary explorations of this topic were several "popular" accounts of human aggression, territoriality, and sexuality as "genetic." Examples of this genre were *African Genesis* (1961) and *The Territorial Imperative* (1966) by Chicago playwright and anthropology aficionado Robert Ardrey, and *The Naked Ape* (1967) by primate zoologist Desmond Morris. Almost all cultural anthropologists and "legitimate" biological anthropologists disputed the claims of these authors as unsupported by science and, in disrespect, dubbed their approach **naked apery.** Nevertheless, in criticizing naked apery as extreme, some anthropologists began wondering what *might* be true about a biological basis for "human nature."

naked apery

Two other anthropologically noteworthy controversies of the 1960s concerned the biological basis of race. The first took place in the early 1960s following publication of biological anthropologist Carleton Coon's book *The Origin of Races* (1963). Coon proposed that five major geographical races of the species *Homo sapiens* had originated in the species *Homo erectus* and evolved into *Homo sapiens* distinctly, the Caucasoid race achieving *sapiens* status first, the Negroid race last. Coon was accused of **scientific racism.** The second controversy took place in the late 1960s when educational psychologist Arthur Jensen proposed that variation in measured intelligence, or IQ, was predominantly genetic in origin, and that the measured average 15-point difference in IQ-test scores between American blacks and whites could never be eliminated by education. In general, anthropologists' objection to this proposition was so strong that the term "Jensenism" became synonymous with "racism" in subsequent debates about the issue. Still, in some quarters of anthropology, the feeling emerged that Jensen was treated unfairly, that his research was rejected for ideological rather than scientific reasons, and that the biological basis for human behavioural differences was a legitimate topic for scientific investigation.

scientific racism

Meanwhile, in the wake of the scientific and political controversies created by Ardrey, Morris, Coon, and Jensen, other developments brought cultural and biological anthropologists closer together. One such development was the promulgation of the **New Physical**

New Physical Anthropology

Anthropology, launched in the 1950s by biological anthropologist Sherwood L. Washburn (b. 1911). The New Physical Anthropology had little to do with the new cultural evolutionism and the New Archaeology launched at approximately the same time. Instead, Washburn encouraged biological anthropologists to understand and accept the synthetic theory of evolution, the synthesis of Darwinism and Mendelian genetics that biologists had achieved in the 1930s. Extended to biological anthropology, the synthesis directed anthropologists to study biological process more than form and to abandon typological thinking, or thinking in terms of fixed, "pure" races. This change in scientific attitude made biological anthropology more acceptable to cultural anthropologists. Meanwhile, biological anthropologists worked out cultural explanations for the geographical distribution of sickle-cell anemia and intolerance of lactose, or milk sugar. These explanatory successes led to the emergence of a new field of **biocultural anthropology**, aimed at exploring interactions between human biology and culture in accordance with the principles of evolutionary ecology. The resulting cooperation between biological and cultural anthropologists primed some anthropologists to be more receptive to the next wave of biological explanations of human behaviour.

    The 1970s saw the emergence, or ascendance, of four bio-behavioural approaches that affected anthropology in varying degrees. The first approach, **medical anthropology**, the cross-cultural and pan-historical study of sickness and health, lacked theoretical unity but also lacked controversy, because its concern with the inheritance of human behaviour was only peripheral. The second approach, **human ethology**, grew out of animal psychology and zoology and involved a more strict commitment to hereditarian concepts such as **fixed action pattern**, **innate releasing mechanism**, and **key stimulus**. Human ethologists examined both the ontogeny, or individual growth, and phylogeny, or evolutionary growth, of biologically-linked behaviours that, in the language of ethology, constituted the **human biogram**. According to ethologists, cultural "universals," like some facial expressions and gestures, were potentially genetic. A diluted form of etholo-

typological thinking

biocultural anthropology

medical anthropology

human ethology

fixed action pattern

innate releasing mechanism

key stimulus

human biogram

gy found its way into the anthropological study of non-verbal communication, or **body language**, in the sciences of **kinesics** and **proxemics**, the studies of body motion and body position. Anthropologists Lionel Tiger and Robin Fox promoted a diluted form of ethology in books like *Men in Groups* (1970) and *The Imperial Animal* (1971), where they expounded their views on "natural" human tendencies. Many critics ended up using the adjective "ethological" to describe *any* proposition that attributed human behaviour to heredity.

body language
kinesics
proxemics

The third bio-behavioural approach to come of age in the 1970s was **behavioural genetics**, the extension of genetic analysis from anatomy and physiology to behaviour, which behavioural geneticists treat as a **phenotype**, or product of gene action. Behavioural geneticists study both "normal" and "abnormal" behavioural phenotypes in order to determine whether they might have either a simple Mendelian or a more complex **polygenic** component. Human behavioural geneticists rely on contrasts of behaviours of twins reared together and apart to help them assign the sources of behavioural differences to nature and nurture. Arthur Jensen's investigation of race, genes, and IQ employed some of these techniques. Behavioural genetics never reached its full potential to provoke controversy in anthropology, because the science is extremely technical and published in journals rarely read by anthropologists.

behavioural genetics

phenotype

polygenic

The bio-behavioural approach that made the greatest inroads in late twentieth-century anthropology was **sociobiology**. This approach became controversial almost immediately after the publication of Edward O. Wilson's landmark book *Sociobiology: The New Synthesis* (1975). Wilson (b. 1929) is a Harvard University entomologist who had been working on the evolutionary problem of altruism, or self-sacrificing behaviours, such as sterile worker ants devoting themselves to helping a queen ant reproduce. The problem with altruism was how to explain it in terms of Darwinian evolution by natural selection. If altruistic behaviour is genetic, it should be subject to the action of natural selection, but the result of such action should be the *reduction* or elimination of the genes responsible. Still, altruism persisted. How? Earlier zoologists had proposed the mechanism of group

sociobiology

selection, whereby individuals sacrifice themselves for the good of groups and then, as group members, benefit indirectly. This mechanism was never entirely convincing, however, so in the early 1970s a number of geneticists proposed the alternative mechanism of **kin selection**. This mechanism became the scientific cornerstone of Wilson's book.

kin selection

Wilson solved the problem of altruism essentially by defining it out of existence. Altruism is not really altruistic; instead, it is "selfish," as Wilson explains with his new concept of **inclusive fitness**. According to Wilson, the genetic basis of most behaviours is polygenic, meaning the result of the action of multiple genes. Genetic relatives share these genes, so individuals who sacrifice themselves can still transmit their sacrificing genes to future generations, as long as they sacrifice themselves for *relatives*. Sociobiology has been called the **biology of nepotism**, an apt nickname, because sociobiologists predict that genes incline individuals to behave more favourably to relatives than to non-relatives, and more favourably to close relatives than to distant relatives. In this way, individuals maximize their inclusive Darwinian fitness and reproductive success. Evolutionary biologist Richard Dawkins (b. 1941) captured many of these ideas in the title of his controversial book *The Selfish Gene* (1976).

inclusive fitness

biology of nepotism

For sociobiology, life is a series of strategic choices in which individuals unconsciously assess the personal costs and benefits of alternative behaviours and end up choosing the alternative with the greatest inclusive yield. Because overall degrees of genetic relatedness can be quantified — parents and children share 50% of their genes, half-siblings 25%, "first" cousins 12.5%, and so forth — sociobiologists can make precise predictions about behaviour and then compare them with empirical reality. To explain altruism among non-relatives, sociobiologist Robert Trivers introduced the supplementary evolutionary mechanism **reciprocal altruism**.

reciprocal altruism

Some of the most controversial pronouncements of sociobiology concern differences between males and females. Both males and females are motivated to maximize their inclusive fitness, but, according to sociobiologists, in fundamentally different ways. In bisexually reproducing species like mammals, males produce a large number of mobile sperm and do not themselves bear children, while females produce a small number of non-mobile eggs and do bear children. These biological differences imply the evolution of behavioural differences. Males are selected to compete for females, because females are a reproductively relevant resource. The reproductive potential of males depends on the number of females they can inseminate. On the other hand, females are selected to resist male advances, because, once inseminated, they cannot become pregnant again until after giving birth. The reproductive potential of females depends on the "quality," not quantity, of male suitors. By depicting males as sexually indiscriminate and females as "choosey," sociobiologists expose themselves to the criticism that they are affirming Western sex-role stereotypes. By proposing that both males and females prefer their "own kind" over "foreigners," sociobiologists expose themselves to the further charges that they are racist and **xenophobic**.

xenophobic

The bulk of Wilson's book focused on insects and other nonhuman animal species. In the final chapter, however, Wilson speculated on how sociobiology might account for at least some of the behaviour of *Homo sapiens*. Within the next few years, he and other sociobiologists refined these speculations and developed a scaled-down, modified version of "human sociobiology." Human sociobiology provoked a storm of opposition in anthropology, where culture was held to be vastly more important than biology as the determinant of behavioural differences. Cultural anthropologists as divergent as cultural materialist Marvin Harris and structuralist Marshall Sahlins united to criticize human sociobiology as erroneous and irrelevant and to condemn it as a disguised ideology of Social Darwinism. This staunch judgement remains the opinion of the majority of cultural anthropologists. At the same time, a small minority of cultural anthropologists, including Yanomamo Indian ethnographer Napoleon Chagnon (b. 1938), has come to adopt the sociobiological perspective. And in primatology, sociobiology has become a dominant research strategy.

Symbolic and Interpretive Anthropology

During the 1960s and 1970s, Max Weber was "rediscovered" by anthropologists, especially in the United States. This rediscovery both reflected and stimulated a new concern for the importance of meaning and the human potential to act creatively in the world. While this had arguably been a concern of cultural anthropologists all along, the essential premise of structuralist theory (in its various guises) was that culture constrained, or controlled, people more than it served, or enabled, them. It was as if people were simply the vehicles for social and psychological structures, and not the other way around. This dominion of structures was unacceptable to a growing number of anthropologists, and yet the "obvious" second option — historical particularism — remained equally unpalatable, mainly for its narrowness of focus and its relative lack of theory. An emerging consensus was that new ways had to be found to explain society and culture without appealing to minutely-controlling social structures or to inaccessible psychological ones. In the 1960s and 1970s, this fresh interest in exploring meaning was expressed in the language of "symbols."

symbolic anthropology

The roots of what came to be called **symbolic anthropology** in Great Britain and **interpretive anthropology** in the United States can be traced back (at least indirectly) to the neo-Kantian philosophy of Wilhelm Dilthey and others, who helped formulate the distinction between the natural sciences, or *naturwissenschaften*, and social sciences, or *geisteswissenschaften*. According to this distinction, promulgated by Franz Boas, the natural sciences deal with entities amenable to generalizations, while the social sciences deal with "mental" entities unique to individuals and groups. To this distinction phenomenologist-philosopher Edmund Husserl (1854-1938) added the observation that natural science is unsuitable for the study of cultural life because cultural life has meaning, which is best understood subjectively as "lived experience."

interpretive anthropology

Husserl's assertions notwithstanding, it would, finally, be difficult to argue that "classical" interpretive and symbolic anthropologists were

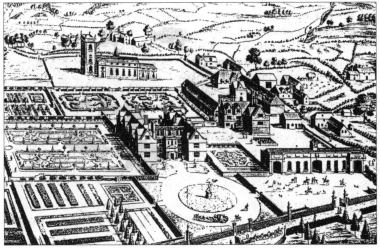

Formal Gardens at Castle Bromwich Hall, West Midlands, England.

From William Dugdale's *History of Warwickshire* (2nd. ed., 1730). A "contextual" interpretation of this eighteenth-century archaeological site is that formal gardens make "statements" about socially accessible and inaccessible space.

inspired by anything less than a desire to do sound empirical research in the best anthropological tradition. What differentiates symbolic and interpretive anthropologists from their colleagues working in explicitly materialist or ecological traditions is their relentless insistence that social and cultural worlds are held together by interpenetrating networks of symbols, each of which is a carrier of cultural meaning. This much, at least, the symbolists and interpretivists have in common. In spite of this underlying similarity, it must be kept in mind that even from the outset, clear differences existed between the two schools, and that these differences both derived from, and had a deep impact on, the respective characters of British and American research.

In Great Britain, the most influential and academically respected symbolic anthropologist was Victor Turner (1920-1983). Turner, like most British anthropologists of his generation, was heavily influenced by Émile Durkheim's dictum that social cohesion was achieved "organically," through the interpenetration of a given society's component parts. Moving beyond the previous generation of structural-functionalists, for whom the essence of "organic solidarity" lay in the concrete institutions and formalized relations of society, Turner focused on the Durkheimian idea that social solidarity is a function of the systems of symbolic logic that connect people. In this way, his "symbolic anthropology" has much in common with Lévi-Strauss' structuralism, similarly inspired by Durkheim. Unlike his French peers (indeed, unlike Durkheim himself), for whom symbolic contrasts and correspondences were seen as a universal mental template on which all culture is built, Turner's main innovations in anthropology derive from his view that social unity is basically *problematic*, and should not be taken for granted. Whereas Durkheim believed that "primitive" humankind came together out of some primordial psychological need for togetherness, Turner argued that people are essentially forced to repeatedly construct social life against those forces in the natural world that constantly threaten to destroy it. Because symbols are the primary vehicles whereby this solidarity is organized, they are instruments, or "tools," employed by people to achieve a particular end — the reproduction of social order.

Beyond this extension of Durkheimian theory, Victor Turner is also credited with breathing fresh life into the ideas of Arnold van Gennep (1873-1957), who, much earlier in the twentieth century, had speculated about the "ritual process." In his work *The Rites of Passage* (1959), van Gennep argued that ritual involves the passage of individuals from one social state to another, and that this entailed three stages: "separation" from the group, "transition" to a new state, and "incorporation" (more properly thought of as "re-incorporation") within the social order. Intrigued by his predecessor's insights, Turner elaborated his concept of ritual to include a theory of process, largely modelled on van Gennep's concept of "liminality." Turner believed

liminal that rituals generate a liminal period in which all notions of social
anti-structure "structure" are undone, and a period of anti-structure ensues. This is what can be observed, for instance, in times of carnival, or during a variety of initiation rites. The ritualized "chaos" of anti-structure involves inverting "normal" identities and roles, so that men are ritually "transformed" into women, kings into servants, and so on. Anti-structure is possible, Turner argued, because the liminal state is one in

which all the limitations of everyday structure are dispensed with, and new creative possibilities opened up. A central aspect of this theory is that, throughout all inversion and liminal transformation of norms and identities, members of a society ultimately come to recognize and reaffirm the basic structural cohesion that they had known all along, in their routine existence outside of ritual. It is by way of this new-found solidarity that society avoids the truly revolutionary implications of the liminal process, and is instead fused in what Turner calls **communitas**.

communitas

In the United States, meanwhile, Clifford Geertz (b.1926) was busily developing his own **semiotic** theory of culture, which also depended on the social circulation and ritual performance of symbols. Whereas Turner derived his core insights from Durkheim, Geertz' intellectual lineage originates with Max Weber, whose emphasis on *meaning*, as opposed to structure, has given Geertz' work a very different orientation from that of his British "counterpart." Taking his cue from Boasian anthropologist Clyde Kluckhohn, Geertz' theory incorporates the idea that at the core of culture is a set of integrated moral values that preserve the correspondence of the world "as it is" with the world "as it should be." The prototypical "interpretive" anthropologist, he set out to show how lived experience is integrated in a coherent, public system of symbols that both renders the world intelligible, and seems uniquely suited to do so. In his enormously influential exposition of the ethnographic method, *The Interpretation of Cultures* (1973), **thick description** is prescribed as the best technique at the ethnographer's disposal for teasing out the **text** of culture, that is, the fine details of human life that make their behaviour intelligible. For Geertz, "man is an animal suspended in webs of significance that he himself has spun." The study of culture is not, therefore, an "experimental science in search of law," but rather "an interpretive one in search of meaning." The meaning Geertz wants to describe is not one locked inside the discrete psychologies of individuals, however, but a network of significations that are on public display. This is particularly the case during rituals like the

semiotic

thick description

text

"Balinese cockfight," in which the social order of Balinese society lurks just below the level of awareness and, embodied in symbols, is collectively shared in by all witnesses to the event.

In the subdiscipline of anthropological archaeology, the interpretive perspective was to find favour during the 1980s as well, especially among those disenchanted with the "excesses" of Lewis Binford's avowedly scientific approach to archaeology. Many archaeologists had been uncomfortable with the so-called New Archaeology and its adherence to key canons of Cartesian rationalism and objectivity. For them, archaeology was allied to history more closely than to science and, because history was a humanity, the **holistic** explanations of Boasian particularism seemed more appropriate than the covering-law model and "economic determinism" of Binford. Some of these archaeologists embraced the viewpoint of **critical anthropologists** that science is elitist and those of French structuralists and structural Marxists that material culture has a symbolic dimension, consciousness causes change, and artifacts reflect social relations as well as adaptation to environments. In the mid-1980s, British archaeologist Ian Hodder codified these views into what he called **contextual**, or "post-processual," archaeology. Echoing the influential French historian Michel Foucault (see the section on postmodernism below), "contextual" refers to Hodder's view that artifacts are embedded in a web of cultural "discourse" that affirms social relations and enhances the power of privileged groups. "Post-processual" refers to his view that the quest to discover law-like processes of culture change, characteristic of the New Archaeology, should be abandoned. Like symbolists and postmodernists in anthropology, post-processualists in archaeology criticized pure scientific objectivity as an unattainable and undesirable theoretical goal. In so doing, they exacerbated divisions within the profession and paved the way for a new wave of nonscientific and anti-scientific critiques.

During the 1960s and 1970s, symbolic and interpretive approaches both expressed and nurtured a growing apprehension within the discipline, namely that those claims to authoritative knowledge that anthropologists had previously taken for granted were at best tenuous

— at least in the cynical environment of the late twentieth-century academy. It is therefore ironic that the same cynicism that cultivated the particularistic, neo-Kantian tendencies in the 1960s and early 1970s also gave rise in the mid-1970s to political economy — a perspective that opposes symbolic and interpretive anthropology in its renewed emphasis on history and objectivity. This was not to be the "old" structuralism of classical British and French approaches, but a new body of thought heavily inspired by the historicism of Marx and Engels. Cultures, the new political economists were to argue, are not merely local but translocal, and are shaped and directed by unequal access to power and material resources. The central problem with symbolic approaches was not that they laid such emphasis on meaning, but that their claims to be doing away with the notion of "structure" were spurious. In fact, political economists insisted, they were busily constructing a new structural orthodoxy in which individual agency still had no real place and in which social change could not really be accommodated.

Whereas both symbolic/interpretive and political economic perspectives are essentially Cartesian, at least to the extent that they continue to assume a theoretical distinction between the observer and the observed, the postmodern "turn" of the 1980s and 1990s has sought to do away even with this distinction. Nevertheless, a reasonable argument can be made that the postmodern paradigm so popular with a current generation of anthropologists has its most immediate anthropological antecedent in those analyses of symbols and meaning pioneered by Turner, Geertz, and archaeologist Hodder.

Political Economy

For anthropologists working in the 1970s, among the most influential of the new perspectives to emerge in sociocultural anthropology was a critical school of thought generally referred to as political economy. As early as the 1950s, anthropologists had been feeling less and less comfortable with the idea that the discipline must study pristine, self-contained, and largely rural communities. In particular, American

Robert Redfield developed a theoretical distinction between the "great tradition" of the literate, religious, and urban to contrast with the "little tradition" of the oral, magical, and rural. However, the connections between the "developed" and "underdeveloped" world remained largely undertheorized until about a decade later. The immediate origins of political economy are traced to the writings of the influential economist Andre Gunder Frank, who began in the 1960s to criticize the agenda of modernization. Frank observed the global capitalist agenda as being more sinister than benign, making dependent satellites of those "developing" nation-states with which the Western world came into contact, and systematically extracting surplus goods and labour in exchange for much less. Underdevelopment was not, in Frank's estimation, a product of local conditions, but the result of progressive capitalist exploitation. Similarly, historian Immanuel Wallerstein identified the historical emergence of a Euro-American "world-economy" in which bourgeois capitalists in the "core" nations of Europe and America appropriate the profits generated by proletarians in the "periphery" — or the rest of the world. Like Frank, Wallerstein understood the proletariat to be trapped in a **world-system** of unequal exchange in which Euro-American society penetrated, politically subjugated, and economically exploited external populations and their produce.

world-system

The emergence of political economy reflects the broader intellectual milieu of the period, to the extent that radical emancipatory social movements such as the counterculture, anti-war, anti-colonial, and feminist movements began to emerge on a large scale in Western society. In the main, the philosophical foundations on which such liberation movements were based originated within the academic world itself, and had a marked impact on the development of intellectual discourse during these decades. For sociocultural anthropology, these trends heralded an upheaval in how the discipline was to regard itself — an intense period of reflection and introspection that has not abated to this day.

It became clear to many practitioners during this period that not only had the discipline failed to problematize the impact of Western colonial and economic imperialism around the world, it had neglected to recognize the essential links between the rise of anthropological knowledge and what has been called the **colonial encounter**. colonial encounter Specifically, nearly all classical ethnographic texts had been written by white Euro-American men, whose work was often made possible by the political and military subjugation of the peoples they studied. In short, many of the remote and exotic communities of the classic ethnographic gaze were captive to, and dependent on, a global system of capitalism and militarism. Anthropologists came to understand, with horror, that their discipline had been the unwitting accomplice of the colonial endeavour, and that it had profited from the oppression of the very peoples whom many well-intentioned ethnographers sought to frame in a sympathetic manner.

Together with the frightening ethical dilemmas that this new awareness precipitated among anthropologists came a growing uneasiness about the implications of this history for orthodox approaches to sociocultural theory. Formulations heavily grounded in a Durkheimian concept of structure or organismic analogy, as were those of British and French anthropologists, were subject to particular scrutiny. In subsequent years, many basic assumptions about the character and truth-value of anthropological knowledge came under attack from various quarters both within the field and without. Among the most strident of anthropological criticisms was that the pristine, timeless, and self-contained organic community of anthropological invention was, in reality, just that — a figment of the ethnographic imagination. A more powerful understanding of human societies, it was argued, would seek to circumvent **Cartesian** assumptions Cartesian of Western bourgeois culture: that there existed an untamed and unchanging, primitive "other" that would undoubtedly benefit from contact with the materially wealthy, the literate, the industrial, and the otherwise "civilized." Similarly, a much cherished notion of the empirical researcher was also called into question. No longer was it taken for granted that the world was easily or dispassionately observed, or that the authors of ethnography were themselves utterly impartial or objective. Seeking to displace these anachronistic perspectives, a number of scholars began to display, rather than conceal or mystify, the various conflicts, class-interests, and arrangements of power and dependency embedded in the history of global capitalism — a history in which anthropology itself had played a role. It was out of this **poststructural** concern for social process, power, conflict, and the origin of **authoritative knowledge** that political economy was born.

Political economy views culture as being shaped within the context of unequal access to wealth and power. Heavily influenced by the writings of Karl Marx, this school may be thought of as materialist because the material conditions of human existence are understood to condition the character of social relations. However, unlike cultural materialism, which views infrastructure (modes of production and reproduction) as a primary determinant of culture, political economy views the material conditions giving rise to these as being grounded in Marxian **ideology**. Because ideologies are constructed systems of ideas, they reflect and perpetuate the specific interests of their authors. For political economy, following Marx, such interests are inscribed in the ways a society differentiates itself according to socioeconomic class, gender, and ethnicity, to name but a few prominent criteria. Whoever controls the means of producing wealth and power, it is argued, also controls conditions for the production of knowledge itself. When knowledge about the world is taken for granted, or unquestioned, it loses its arbitrary character and comes to be seen as "natural." Ideology at this stage ceases merely to embody the interests of one group within society, and becomes a dominant perspective of the society — taken for granted by the powerful and powerless alike. Unchallenged dominant ideologies, such as that cluster of heterogeneous meanings and activities that make up global capitalism, recapitulate the economic and political interests of some while simultaneously "mystifying" this essential inequality in power-relations for others. Political economists refer to this mystification as **hegemony**.

In the hands of political economists, the concept of culture is reconceived. No longer thought of as immaterial or metaphysical, culture becomes a system of objective and concrete forces, or ideologies, to be studied. No longer perceiving culture as a unified and undifferentiated object of study, a recent generation of theorists has indicated that even the existence of culture is not to be assumed. Rather, it is problematic. Under what social and historical conditions do particular interests and activities come to exist? Furthermore, how do they interpenetrate to create new meanings and practices, and how are these received, accepted, modified or resisted by others? In practice, anthropologists persuaded by this approach have moved the discipline away from the community studies of earlier generations. While these viewed cultures as timeless, exotic, and autonomous, theorists during the 1970s and 1980s looked at the effects on local societies of the "penetration" of large-scale regional, national, and international political-economic forces, such as global capitalism. Eric Wolf (b.1923), Sidney Mintz (b.1922), and William Roseberry (b.1950) stand out as prominent anthropologists who have worked to illuminate these issues over the past quarter-century.

The effort within political economy to understand the interpenetration of global and local processes certainly illuminated the changing and malleable character of culture, but for many this raised more questions than it answered. Among the most troublesome: if past ethnographic representations of the exotic "other" did not so much reflect objective reality as further the norms, values, and assumptions of Western society (i.e., that there were indeed primitive and timeless cultures in dire need of civilizing), how was a new generation of cultural anthropologists to liberate itself from ethnocentrism and still construct accurate and meaningful accounts of cultures which, in the final analysis, were still very different from those of Euro-American scholars? Grounded as it was in Marx' political philosophy, even political economy could ultimately be read as ethnocentric, because it insists that culture is the product of materialist power struggles — a uniquely Western form of analysis. Anthropologists began to question whether it was even desirable, let alone ethical, to continue to seek any one cause or configuration of causes that determine culture, given the historical connections between industrial capitalism, colonialism, and the post-Enlightenment ideal of scientific progress. These questions are significant because they cut to the very heart of what anthropology attempts to do: devise powerful and parsimonious models that explain how people interact with each other and the world. As most cultural anthropologists came to realize, however, extracting anthropology from its "modernist" heritage — a heritage that divides the world into the Cartesian oppositions of subject and object, self and other, rational and irrational, and culture and nature, among others — would prove extraordinarily difficult.

Postmodernism

While political economy hastened the demise of the traditional anthropological picture of society and culture, the advent of post-modernism in the social sciences and humanities is often credited with "exploding" the culture concept once and for all. While this is perhaps an exaggeration, it is certain that the theoretical concerns that ethnographers began to express during the 1960s and 1970s — concerns that political economists sought to address — were not easily resolved. While not properly labelled a homogenous "movement" as such, postmodernists working within a variety of disciplines have certainly shared a perspective that emphasizes the subjectivity of experience and, consequently, the impossibility of any one form of authoritative knowledge. In anthropology, the postmodern turn had the effect of advancing and refining debate over the theoretical and ethical issues first raised by political economists.

The modernist agenda is not easily dispensed with, precisely because it is embodied in key Western assumptions about an objective world that can and should be subdued and controlled — politically, economically, and ideologically — by the orderly, dispassionate, and

philosophical anarchist · rational Europeans. An early critic of modernism was **philosophical anarchist** Paul Feyerband, who argued that there is no logical way to

paradigms · choose between conventional scholarly models, or **paradigms**. The concept of paradigms came from historian and philosopher-of-science Thomas Kuhn, who in his highly influential book *The Structure of Scientific Revolutions* (1962) argued that science is not cumulative, that it does not necessarily progress toward clearer understanding and Truth. Instead, science is conventional, consisting of answers to questions that scientists agree are appropriate to ask at a particular time and place. For a while, according to Kuhn, this period of "normal" science yields results, but, eventually, noncomforming observations instigate scientific "revolutions" whereby old questions are superseded by new questions, to which the observations conform. A new period of normal science ensues, until other nonconforming observations instigate another scientific revolution. Kuhn called the intellectual framework for normal science a "paradigm," and the process of scientific revolution a "paradigm shift," citing as his main example the shift from Aristotelian to Newtonian science in the Scientific Revolution of the seventeenth century. His main point was that new paradigms are not necessarily superior to old ones; paradigms are merely different and incommensurable.

Feyerband argued that there is no logical way to choose between paradigms because all such explanations are inevitably *interpretations*. Scientific thought and institutions, like any others, are the products of lived experience, as are their assumptions about the "truth," or authoritative nature, of their special knowledge. The truth-claims of scientists, Feyerband insisted, cannot therefore be understood as superior to other manners of explanation for social phenomena — rather, *all* explanations are basically incommensurable. Likewise, an important insight of anthropologists in recent years has been that modernity has carried forward these ideals since at least the sixteenth century. The recognition has been that this project is *itself* an historical event. The modernist perspective itself constitutes an **invented tradition** — invented tradition the product of creative social action through time and *not* a "revelation" or awakening to true understanding of an external, objective reality. This revolution in perspective has caused both great excitement and upheaval in the humanities and social sciences. While a number of scholars stand out as having made profound contributions to developing a "postmodern" perspective (Antonio Gramsci, Anthony Giddens, and Raymond Williams, for instance), two in particular have directly influenced the course of anthropological theory,

and deserve brief mention here: the French social theorists Michel
Foucault and Pierre Bourdieu.[1]

Writing in the 1970s, Michel Foucault (1926-1984), a historian of
culture, viewed social institutions and relationships as being intimate-
ly grounded in a pervasive economy of **discourses of power** which
shape relations between people at all levels in a society. In his formulation, "power" ceased to be solely a function of formal political institutions and became something inscribed in everyday life. The many
different roles played by individuals (employers, employees, doctors,
patients, men, women, priests, faithful, teachers, students, etc.) all bear
the stamp of certain kinds of relations between people in which some
dominate and others are subjugated. Whoever dominates these relationships, Foucault argued, also controls the economic and ideological conditions under which "knowledge" or "truth" (and therefore
"reality") are defined. Dominating classes inscribe their power, in
Foucault's scenario, in and through a series of tactics and strategies
that instruct people to "be" a certain way in the world. In this way,
beginning with the Enlightenment and the rise of the nation-state in
the eighteenth century, discourses of science, sexuality, and humanism
became dominant in European society, preserving their power
through mechanisms of control such as prisons, hospitals, asylums,
and museums. Foucault's central contribution to postmodern social
theory has been to show how power determines different social
forms through history. Because modernity is viewed, alongside other
configurations of knowledge, as the product of power, the objective
character of scientific knowledge is shown to be an historical construct.

Addressing similar issues relating to power and domination, but
coming at the problem from another angle, Pierre Bourdieu (b. 1930)
has worked during the 1970s and 1980s to develop a theory that
places the social actor at the centre of social process. Unlike Foucault,
whose theory views individuals and their interrelationships as being
determined by discourses of power, Bourdieu holds that these same
persons and social arrangements are created by human agents who

discourses of power

assemble their cultures through **practice**, or **praxis**. What people "do" _practice_
in practice is create, reproduce, and change a variety of "taxonomies" _praxis_
that are understood to be the basis of social relations. These taxonomies are made up of symbolic representations that do not merely
reflect ideas about the world, but actually _make the world_ what it is for
the people who live in it. Individuals are powerful to the extent that
they can _impose_ on others taxonomies that reproduce their own
power and authority, and are powerless to the extent that they are
unable to escape their social positioning in relation to the taxonomies
created by others. Either way, the taxonomies wielded by the powerful in relation to the powerless are only relevant insofar as they are
lodged within a configuration of social relations.

The notion of the "relational" is so significant in Bourdieu's
thought because it helps to move social science away from those various formulations of social structure as conceived by an earlier generation of Durkheimian thinkers. For Bourdieu, "structures" and "cultures" are not to be compared to machines or organisms, because culture and society are ultimately not things but systems of relationships
— or **fields**. Bourdieu has defined fields as fluid, open-ended "net- _fields_
works" of "objective relations between positions." Complex societies,
he has argued, are comprised of any number of fields (i.e., artistic,
intellectual, economic, religious, etc.) which, although co-existing
spatially and temporally, are nevertheless discrete and integrated
according to their own internal "logics." Within fields, the total
imposition of one group's set of taxonomies upon another's results in
the production of a "natural" order, or **doxa**, in which the essentially _doxa_
arbitrary character of the "powerful" taxonomies is obscured. What
emerges, for the powerful and powerless alike, is a sense that certain
thoughts, feelings, and actions are part of the outer, objective world,
while others (those of the dominated) are "unnatural."

In short, social relations that come to be taken for granted are
actually the result of one interest group's symbolic domination of
others within a society. What is seen to be "real" in any society, from
Bourdieu's perspective, inevitably reflects the point of view of who-

ever's interests are served *by* that reality. However, unlike Foucault's model, in which individuals are dominated by a powerful system, Bourdieu believes that individual actors are able to create alternative taxonomies that resist those that the powerful seek to impose. The

habitus wellspring of this individual agency is the **habitus**, or the ways in which personal history and social positioning allow individuals to improvise or innovate.

Throughout the 1980s and 1990s, Foucault's and Bourdieu's ideas have had a dramatic impact on anthropological theory. Depending on one's sympathies, their work has been highly illuminating or deeply mystifying. In either case, it is clear that for many researchers, suddenly there seemed no centre, no firm ground from which students of human life could gaze objectively at their subject matter. Henceforth no "truth" would be taken for granted and no perspective left

deconstruction unchallenged. **Deconstruction** became a new watchword for anthropologists, because the sanguine ambition of positivism to explain the world was no longer seen as a possibility. On the contrary, to be a "vulgar" positivist was to be misguided or naive, because it was not the culture itself that needed explaining, so much as the anthropologist's explanation of that culture. It was the representation or account of a people, in other words, that required understanding, or deconstruction, because discrete cultures as "objects" are only apprehended at all through such accounts. Some have mistakenly taken this to mean that postmodernism denies the existence of objective reality,

solipsism and have thereby accused postmodernist researchers of **solipsism**. It is ironic, however, that the postmodern perspective in effect recapitulates an idea that had been prominent in anthropology since Boas and his students first championed the cause of cultural relativism in the first decades of the twentieth century: that culture mediates and conditions all knowledge of the world, like a lens. In this way, while it is clear that a world truly does exist independently of how we know it, it is equally clear that there is no perspective, scientific or otherwise, that is not in the last instance rooted in particular histories and biases — an integral feature, seemingly, of our common humanity.

In anthropology, the postmodern perspective has been most

influential in the writing of ethnography. Anthropologists working in the 1980s and 1990s have thus been extremely conscious of the subjective nature of the documents they produce. James Clifford and George Marcus' edited volume *Writing Culture: The Poetics and Politics of Ethnography* (1986) has been particularly influential in advancing the ideas that cultural accounts are constructed "texts," and that the relations between the writer, reader, and subject matter of ethnography are complex and problematic. Whereas "standard" interpretive approaches would view subjects as creative actors busily "constructing" their social worlds out of symbols, postmodernists have noted with deep irony that these same ethnographers privilege their own status as external observers. In other words, while everybody else was evidently forced to build culture, anthropologists were exempt from this process: it was for them to observe, rather than to be observed. In contrast, postmodernism argues that ethnographies, no less than any other form of creative writing, are texts that privilege the perspective of their authors. This insight has had deep implications for anthropological theory. Because the account being produced most often comes from a particular viewpoint — that of the white, middle-class, educated Euro-American male — it reflects and asserts (albeit implicitly) the concerns and interests of its author. True objectivity is hardly possible, because even if the researcher deliberately adopted a non-stereotypical object of study, he would still have little choice but to employ the analytical categories and concerns explicitly and implicitly fashioned by the academy and (more broadly) the society in which the knowledge he "possesses" has been formed. It is that which goes unquestioned — the division of the ethnographic project into subject and object — that betrays the subtle yet powerful influence of modernity on anthropological theory.

Recognizing the impossibility of pure objectivity, a recent generation of ethnographers has attempted to circumnavigate the ethical and methodological dilemmas raised by postmodern theory. They have done so by looking for ways in which to describe different cultures and societies *without* denying the subjectivity of the people being analyzed, and *without* laying claim to absolute, or authoritative, knowledge about them. Needless to say, given that anthropology has been suffused with and directed by modernist concerns, this lofty ambition is easier proclaimed than accomplished. Heavily influenced by the writings of Foucault and Bourdieu, one popular strategy has thus been to show how the subjects of ethnography themselves set about creating and negotiating the categories of meaning that inform their social worlds. Often labelled **social constructionism**, after a phrase popularized by sociologists Peter Berger and Thomas Luckman in the 1960s, this methodology attempts to demonstrate how ethnographic subjects employ language and patterned activity to create, sustain, and change cultural meaning, and continues (at least implicitly) to be highly influential in anthropological writing today. More recently, scholars have elaborated on this form of analysis to highlight the essentially contingent nature of cultural meaning. In his work *Imagined Communities* (1983), for instance, Benedict Anderson reconstructs the concept of the nation-state from the ground up, effectively arguing that nations are "imagined" into being under particular sets of social and historical conditions (such as the post-medieval influence of print-media and its marked impact on European vernacular languages). Likewise, *The Invention of Tradition* (1992), edited by Eric Hobsbawm and Terence Ranger, is a collection of historical essays that point to the recent, "invented" origins of traditions and practices that are often portrayed as being ancient markers of ethnic identity. In this vein, much attention has been focused within anthropology in recent years on understanding how different forms of human community, such as those identified according to social positioning (i.e., according to such criteria as socioeconomic class, race, ethnicity, and gender) are constructed in and inscribed on a wide variety of historical contexts.

social constructionism

Conclusion

In anthropology today, on the threshold of the twenty-first century, the voices of postmodernists arise from a camp of humanists whose tents are pitched alongside the tents of would-be scientists. The dialogue between these two camps reflects a desire to negotiate a set of theoretical priorities that will please at least most anthropologists most of the time. This task will prove challenging, because, as a group, anthropologists are characteristically opinionated and diverse. If the essential unity of the field is to be preserved, or reclaimed, any theoretical consensus must include physical anthropologists, archaeological anthropologists, linguistic anthropologists, and an especially outspoken and diverse subfield of cultural anthropologists, all divided into numerous special interest groups. What can the history of anthropological theory show those anthropologists, and students of anthropology, who want to go beyond "celebrating" theoretical diversity and find some common ground?

It can show them that anthropologists are united at least by their own history. Simply put, they are a product of their past. There is, of course, no *one* anthropological past, but the amount of accumulated common experience is sufficient to serve as a basis for identifying unifying themes. Anthropologists in particular should know that a "dialogue with the ancestors" (in this book, some still living) can help accomplish such a task. In certain historical episodes, anthropology appears to have "reinvented" itself, as when, for example, Franz Boas sought to purge anthropology of racism or when, later, cultural neo-evolutionists and New Archaeologists sought to return anthropology to nomothetic science. Nevertheless, just because past theorists have *reacted* to earlier theorists, rather than perpetuated their views, it does not necessarily follow that the history of anthropological theory lacks pattern and coherence. On the contrary, to search for pattern and coherence in the history of anthropological theory would be a meaningful way for readers of this book to figure out what it all adds up to for them.

One undeniable feature of the history of anthropological theory is that it is embedded in Western experience. Only the most naive reader of this book would be able to conclude that theory is "out there," ready to be plucked from the air by a particularly ingenious or fortuitous "discoverer." By adopting the analytical distinctions among religion, science, and humanism, we have seen clearly, in hindsight, that the various ancient and medieval schools leading up to Christianity have had a profound and lasting influence on the development of anthropological theory, as have the revival of humanism in the Renaissance and the origin of modern science in the seventeenth century. Arguably, the most momentous historical episode of all has been the voyages of geographical discovery, which brought Westerners into contact with non-Westerners and launched the period of cross-cultural reflection that, in one way or another, has characterized anthropology ever since. Even in physical and archaeological anthropology, the subsequent history of the field from the eighteenth through the twentieth centuries is replete with examples of how theory is situated, or "contextualized," in particular times and places. More than one historian of theory has been caught wondering, at least privately, "Will the real truth please stand up?"

Sometimes courses in the history of anthropological theory — especially those dubbed "one dead guy a week" — are taught by the "trapeze method," meaning swinging from one theory to another over time. The links among theories established by this method are, at best, superficial, and, worse, give the false impression that theories float above real people like acrobats who never touch ground. In fact, theories are very real. That is why they are buffeted by history and subject to human device.

Note

1   Although we pay special attention to Foucault and Bourdieu within the section on "postmodernists," it is only fair to point out that neither theorist has identified his own work with that of "radical" post-structuralists within cultural anthropology. In fact, Foucault has been faulted by some for what has been taken to be an overly structural approach that does little to account for social change, while Bourdieu has gone to some pains to distance his work from that of those nihilistically-minded cultural interpretivists and deconstructionists who deny outright the possibility of objectivity in social science. Rejecting this proposition, Bourdieu has

felicitously, if cynically, dubbed this philosophy within anthropology the "diary disease." We feel justified in including discussions of Foucault's and Bourdieu's respective work not, therefore, because they can or should be thought of as "postmodern" in narrow terms. Rather, we view their contributions to theorizing such concepts as power, resistance, and agency as important influences on a recent generation of cultural anthropologists.

review questions

Introduction to Anthropology

1. What are the four traditional subdisciplines of anthropology? What has happened to these subdisciplines in the late twentieth century?
2. Why can there be no *one* history of anthropological theory?
3. What are the differences among scientific, humanistic, and religious systems of thought?

Anthropology in Antiquity

4. What did the pre-Socratic philosophers contribute to anthropological theory?
5. What are the differences between the Platonic and Aristotelian legacies to anthropology?
6. How did Stoicism bridge Greek and Roman thought?
7. What were the tenets of Augustinian Christianity? How did they affect anthropology in the Middle Ages?

The Middle Ages

8. In the period of the Middle Ages, what did Islam contribute to anthropology?
9. What were the differences between the theologies of Saint Augustine and Saint Thomas Aquinas? How did these

differences affect the history of anthropological theory?

The Renaissance

10. What *was* the Renaissance?
11. ·What was the Renaissance legacy to anthropological theory?

Voyages of Geographical Discovery

12. Why were the voyages of geographical discovery so important in the history of anthropological theory?
13. What is the significance of the difference between the portrayals of native peoples as natural slaves and as natural children?
14. What are the differences between monogenesis and polygenesis?

The Scientific Revolution

15. What is the difference between deduction, associated with French rationalism, and induction, associated with British empiricism?
16. What roles did Nicholaus Copernicus, Tycho Brahe, Johann Kepler, and Galileo Galilei play in the Scientific Revolution?
17. How did medieval cosmology differ from the cosmology of Isaac Newton?
18. How did the Scientific Revolution affect the history of anthropological theory?

The Enlightenment

19. What are the differences between deists and theists?
20. What is the anthropological significance of John Locke's concept of *tabula rasa*?
21. Who were the universal historians? How were they anthropological?

The Rise of Positivism

22. In the early nineteenth century, what were the intellectual reactions to the French Revolution?
23. What was Auguste Comte's philosophy of Positivism? How did it integrate social dynamics and statics?
24. What is the significance of positivism for the history of anthropological theory?

Marxism

25. In dialectical materialism, how did Karl Marx and Friedrich Engels change the philosophy of Friedrich Hegel?
26. What is the labour theory of value?
27. On what basis did Marx and Engels predict the inevitable future collapse of capitalism?
28. What does it mean to be a Marxist anthropologist?

Classical Cultural Evolutionism

29. How did the formulations of nineteenth-century cultural evolutionists differ from the formulations of eighteenth-century universal historians?
30. How did Lewis Henry Morgan explain the evolution of marriage, family, and sociopolitical organization? How did other evolutionists disagree with his explanation?
31. According to a synthesis of the views of Edward Burnett Tylor and Herbert Spencer, how did magico-religious beliefs and institutions evolve?
32. How did James Frazer differentiate magic, religion, and science?

Evolutionism vs. Diffusionism

33. How do diffusionism and evolutionism differ as explanations of culture change?

34. What were the differences between the heliocentric and *kulturkreise* versions of diffusionism?
35. What does the doctrine of psychic unity have to do with the difference between evolutionism and diffusionism?

Archaeology Comes of Age

36. In the nineteenth century, what developments led to scientific acceptance of the idea of prehistory?
37. In the nineteenth century, how was archaeology linked to racism and colonialism?

Darwinism

38. What was the basis of the debate between Neptunist and Vulcanist geologists?
39. What was the basis of the debate between uniformitarian and catastrophist geologists?
40. What were the major influences on Charles Darwin's theory of evolution?
41. How did Darwin's mechanism of natural selection differ from Jean Lamarck's mechanism of the inheritance of acquired characteristics?
42. Why is the term Social Darwinism historically misleading?
43. What kinds of moral systems have been based on Darwinian biology?

Franz Boas

44. How did Franz Boas' intellectual background shape his anthropology?
45. What is historical particularism?
46. What kind of influence did Boas exert in anthropology?

Robert Lowie and Alfred Louis Kroeber

47. In what ways did Robert Lowie remain true to Boasian anthropology?
48. How did Alfred Louis Kroeber depart from Boasian anthropology?

Margaret Mead and Ruth Benedict

49. Why did Margaret Mead undertake anthropological research in Samoa? What were her research findings? What does Derek Freeman think about them?
50. What did Ruth Benedict write about in *Patterns of Culture*?
51. How did Mead and Benedict change the intellectual orientation of Boasian anthropology?

The Influence of Sigmund Freud

52. How did Sigmund Freud come to the realization that people have a subconscious? How did he differentiate the id, ego, and superego?
53. How did Freud explain the origin of the psychic conflict that (according to him) plagued humankind?
54. How did Freud characterize human nature?

Development of Psychological Anthropology

55. In what ways was Freudian psychology in theoretical conflict with Boasian anthropology?
56. In psychodynamic anthropology, how were culture and personality related?
57. How did Cora Du Bois study the Alorese psychodynamically?
58. How did John Whiting and Irvin Child attempt to make psychological anthropology rigorous?

The Influence of Émile Durkheim

59. According to Émile Durkheim, what is the distinction between mechanical and organic solidarity?
60. What did Durkheim mean by social facts, the collective consciousness, and collective representations?
61. How do the concepts of "sacred" and "profane" relate to Durkheim's theory of religion, and what is the role of the "totem?"
62. How did Durkheim's vision of society differ from the vision of Karl Marx?

French Structural Anthropology

63. What is the relationship among the theories of Émile Durkheim, Marcel Mauss, and Claude Lévi-Strauss?
64. How do the concepts of binary opposition and exchange figure in Lévi-Strauss' structural analysis of kinship?
65. What is structural Marxism?
66. What was the basis of the disagreement between economic formalists and substantivists?

British Social Anthropology

67. What is the organismic analogy? What is its significance for anthropology?
68. What did Alfred Reginald Radcliffe-Brown mean by functionalism, structuralism, and structural-functionalism?
69. What was Bronislaw Malinowski's theory of functionalism? How did his theory differ from that of Radcliffe-Brown?
70. How did Africa figure in British social anthropology?
71. Besides Radcliffe-Brown and Malinowski, who else made contributions to British social anthropology? What contributions did they make?

The Legacy of Max Weber

72. How was "Weberian" analysis different from that of Weber's contemporaries, especially Marx and Durkheim? What was its central contribution to understanding the nature of "culture?"
73. What role did religion play in Weber's analysis? Which religion best represents the theory he developed and why?
74. How does Weber elaborate a theory of human "agency"? What is "rationalization," and why is the "charismatic prophet" central to Weber's thinking?
75. Describe the impact of Max Weber on subsequent generations of anthropologists. What aspects of his thought have been influential on more contemporary researchers such as A. F. C. Wallace and Jean and John Comaroff?

Cognitive Anthropology

76. What is the difference between emics and etics? How does the difference derive from the study of language?
77. What is the Sapir-Whorf hypothesis?
78. What methods and concepts are employed in cognitive anthropology?

Cultural Neo-Evolutionism

79. How does thermodynamics figure in Leslie White's science of culturology?
80. How did Julian Steward differentiate multilineal, unilineal, and universal versions of cultural evolutionism?
81. How did Marshall Sahlins and Elman Service reconcile the evolutionary views of White and Steward?
82. What do cultural neo-evolutionism and the New Archaeology have in common?

Cultural Materialism

83. How do the distinctions between emics and etics and between mental and behavioural perspectives figure in cultural materialism?
84. What is the principle of infrastructural determinism? Why does Marvin Harris prefer it?

Biologized Anthropology

85. What developments led to the emergence of biological approaches to human behaviour in the 1970s?
86. What are the assumptions and goals of human ethology and human behavioural genetics?
87. What is the sociobiological solution to the problem of the evolution of altruism?
88. How does sociobiology explain differences between females and males?
89. What are some opinions about the applicability of sociobiology to anthropology?

Symbolic and Interpretive Anthropology

90. Out of which intellectual traditions did symbolic and interpretive approaches emerge? Against which theoretical schools in anthropology were they a reaction?
91. Compare and contrast Victor Turner's application of Durkheim's ideas with that of structural-functionalists. What were some central differences between them?
92. What made Clifford Geertz' "interpretive" anthropology distinct from Victor Turner's "symbolic" anthropology? How are symbols differently conceived by either theorist?
93. How did Ian Hodder's "contextual" approach to archaeology differ from the "New Archaeology" of Lewis Binford? Are there any thematic similarities between contextual archaeology and

parallel developments in sociocultural anthropology?

Political Economy

94. Characterize the intellectual, social, and political climate in which political economy first took root. What impact did these characteristics have on anthropological theory?
95. What is the "world system" and how does it relate to the "colonial encounter"?
96. What objections did political economists have to "Cartesian" forms of analysis?
97. Describe the relationship between the ideas of Karl Marx and those of political economists. What are "material" forces in political economic terms and how do they create "hegemony"?

Postmodernism

98. Why is the concept of "subjectivity" so important in postmodern thought? Why do anthropologists in this tradition reject the project of "modernity"?
99. Michel Foucault viewed history as being suffused with and by discourses of "power" and "knowledge." In his formulation, what is the role attributed to these discourses in generating different forms of social relationships?
100. Pierre Bourdieu has employed the concepts of "practice" and "habitus" to show how social life is created, sustained, and changed. Define these terms and describe their place in Bourdieu's theory.
101. Various contemporary anthropologists have been influenced by "schools" of thought often lumped together under the rubric "social constructionism." What is social constructionism and what importance do many of its advocates attach to the related concepts of the "invented tradition" and the "imagined community"?

glossary

This glossary provides definitions of **boldfaced** terms. If a definition contains another defined term, it too is boldfaced.

adaptation In **cultural ecology**, the result of cultures adjusting to environments; in Darwinian evolution, the result of **natural selection**.

adhesions Edward Burnett Tylor's name for cultural traits that are significantly associated.

agency In recent anthropological theory, creative acts of intentioned individuals that generate social form and meaning.

altruism Self-sacrificing behaviour. See **group selection** and **kin selection**.

ancestor worship The veneration of departed relatives, in **classical cultural evolutionism** a religious phase.

anima An invisible and diffuse supernatural force that can take the form of souls and ghosts.

anomie In Durkheimian social analysis, the sense of personal alienation caused by the absence of familiar social norms.

anthropo-geography The doctrine of Friedrich Ratzel, who analyzed relationships among geographically contiguous cultures, opposing psychic unity.

antipodes Opposites, or peoples on opposite sides of the world.

anti-structure According to Victor Turner, the side of culture expressed through ritual "chaos," as during liminal states.

armchair anthropologist An anthropologist who has done little or no fieldwork.

authoritative knowledge The idea that one body of knowledge and understanding is privileged over other bodies, in that it has greater access to ultimate reality or the "Truth."

band The simplest form of human social organization, placed in evolutionary sequence before the tribe, chiefdom, and state.

basic personality structure In psychodynamic anthropology, core personality, shaped by primary cultural institutions and projected onto secondary cultural institutions.

behavioural genetics The branch of genetics concerned with genetic contributions to behavioural differences. See phenotype and polygenic.

binary oppositions In French structural anthropology, the universal logic of dualities.

binomial nomenclature The hierarchical system of classifying all living things into groups with scientific names, including one name for genus and a second name for species.

biocultural anthropology Anthropology aimed at exploring interactions between human biology and culture in accordance with the principles of ecology.

biogenetic law The nineteenth-century evolutionary principle that ontogeny, the growth of an individual, recapitulates phylogeny, the growth of a species.

biology of nepotism A colloquial label for sociobiology, focusing on kin selection.

body language A colloquial term for non-verbal communication.

bourgeoisie In Marxism, the middle class.

British empiricism The intellectual tradition associated with philosophers Francis Bacon and John Locke and the epistemology of induction.

British social anthropology The school led by Alfred Reginald Radcliffe-Brown and Bronislaw Malinowski and espousing structuralism, functionalism, and structural-functionalism.

Calvinist Protestantism The diverse body of Christian doctrine and practice whose origins are traced to the teachings of John Calvin, opposing Roman Catholic claims to authority and believing in a Christianity based on the verbal inspiration of scripture and the "justification by Faith."

Cartesian Referring to the view of French philosopher René Descartes that there is a radical dualism between mind and matter, body and soul, subject and object.

catastrophism Contrasted with uniformitarianism, the geological doctrine that agents of geological change have been more dramatic in the past than in the present.

cephalic index The measured ratio of head breadth to head length, used in nineteenth-century racial classifications.

charismatic prophets As identified by Max Weber, individuals who, having endured some episode of extreme physical or emotional duress, experience a revelation, typically in the form of a dream or vision, that mandates the establishment of a new social order based on new ethical ideals and behaviours.

classical cultural evolutionism The theoretical orientation of nine-teenth-century cultural evolutionists who used the comparative method.

classificatory A type of kinship system that, contrasted with the descriptive type, "lumps" kinship categories.

cognitive anthropology The school of anthropology concerned with folk taxonomies and semantic domains. See ethnoscience, ethnolinguistics, and New Ethnography.

collective consciousness In Durkheimian social theory, the source of collective representations or social facts, sometimes called the group mind.

collective representations In Durkheimian social theory, manifestations of the collective consciousness or group mind.

colonial encounter The historical encounter between European explorers and colonizers and the indigenous peoples of the world who were often politically and economically marginalized or oppressed by colonialism.

communitas A term employed by Victor Turner to refer to the ritual fusion of individuals into a collective identity.

comparative method The use of extant primitive peoples to represent extinct primitive peoples, as in classical cultural evolutionism.

componential analysis A major method of cognitive anthropology, used to generate folk taxonomies of a semantic domain.

configurationalism The search for cultural patterns, often in the idiom of psychology.

consanguine A family type based on group marriage between brothers and sisters.

contextual The archaeology of post-processualists, critical of nomothetic New Archaeology.

contract societies In the schema of Henry Maine, societies that stressed individualism, held property in private, and maintained control by legal sanctions, contrasted with status societies.

cosmological order A phrase employed in religion to describe the nature of otherworldly deities, or powers, and their relationships to human beings.

cosmology The branch of philosophy concerned with the origin and structure of the universe.

creationism The view that species are divinely created and do not evolve.

criterion of form A tenet of nineteenth-century anthropo-geography and diffusionism.

critical anthropologists Anthropologists who share criticisms of positivism.

cross-cousins Cousins related through parents of the opposite sex. See matrilateral cross-cousin marriage and patrilateral cross-cousin marriage.

cross-cultural analysis Analysis of cultural similarities and differences.

cultural ecology Examinations of interactions between cultural and environmental variables. See adaptation.

cultural materialism A theoretical orientation that distinguishes emic from etic perspectives and mental from behavioural domains, advocating infrastructural determinism.

cultural neo-evolutionism Twentieth-century cultural evolutionism, a revival and reformulation of classical cultural evolutionism.

cultural relativism The proposition that cultural differences should not be judged by absolute standards.

culture area A geographical area associated with a culture.

culture-at-a-distance A focus of American psychological anthropology in the era of the Second World War.

culture circle Translated "kulturkreis," a concept central to some versions of diffusionism.

culture-historical archaeology Archaeology in the era of Boasian historical particularism.

culturology Leslie White's name for the nomothetic study of culture.

Darwinism A loosely used term identifying ideas associated with Charles Darwin's theory of evolution.

deconstruction A term describing the ambition of postmodernism to understand the political and cultural contexts "hidden" behind the writing, or "construction," of philosophical, literary, historical, and ethnographic narratives.

deduction In scientific **epistemology**, the use of logic to reason from general to particular statements. Contrast with **induction**.

deistic Pertaining to deism, the view that God created the universe but remains relatively uninvolved in its day-to-day operations. Contrast with **theistic**.

descriptive A type of kinship system that, contrasted with the **classificatory** type, "splits" kinship categories.

diachronic Historical, concerned with the past. Contrast with **synchronic**.

dialectical In the Marxist theory of **dialectical materialism**, philosopher Friedrich Hegel's formulation of change as **thesis-antithesis-synthesis**.

dialectical materialism The philosophy of Karl Marx and Friedrich Engels, commonly called **Marxism**.

dictatorship of the proletariat In **dialectical materialism**, the temporary phase of political organization preceding permanent communism.

diffusionism The doctrine that cultural innovations evolve once and are then acquired through borrowing or immigration. Contrast with **independent invention**.

discourses of power A phrase coined by French social theorist Michel Foucault to describe the heterogeneous spectrum of institutions, rhetorics, tactics, and strategies employed by one group to dominate another group ideologically, politically, and economically.

DNA Deoxyribonucleic acid, the biochemical substance of heredity.

doxa A term used by French social theorist Pierre Bourdieu to describe a state in which all members of a community take for granted the "naturalness" of relations within that community, regardless of social, economic, and political inequities.

eclectics According to cultural materialism, anthropologists who are sometimes cultural materialists and other times cultural idealists. See infrastructural determinism.

ego Translated "I," according to Sigmund Freud, the part of the psyche that interacts with the outside world.

Electra complex According to Sigmund Freud, the troublesome psychological state of girls induced by their sexual desire for their fathers. Contrast with Oedipus complex.

elementary forms For Émile Durkheim, the equivalent of collective representations, similar to elementary structures.

elementary structures In French structural anthropology, universal mental logics and their cultural manifestations.

emic Derived from phonemic, the epistemological perspective of the investigated, or "the inside point of view." Contrast with etic.

enculturation The process of an individual acquiring culture, usually while growing up.

Enlightenment The period of eighteenth-century intellectual history preceding the French Revolution.

entropy Disorder in the universe, increasing according to the second law of thermodynamics.

epistemology The branch of philosophy that explores the nature of knowledge.

ethical Pertaining to correct conduct or behaviour, prescribing in advance what actions should be undertaken, or attitudes and beliefs adopted, in order to put oneself in accordance with a metaphysical order.

ethnocentric Pertaining to ethnocentrism, or cultural bias.

ethnolinguistics The approach derived from the linguistically-oriented methods of cognitive anthropology.

ethnoscience A term for the collection of methods used in cognitive anthropology.

ethos Spiritual character, used by some anthropologists to characterize culture.

etic Derived from phonetic, the epistemological perspective of the investigator, or "the outside point of view." Contrast with emic.

Eurocentric The implicit and explicit rating of non-European societies and cultures according to a generalized European scale of norms and values, usually excluding those former colonies settled by Europeans and peopled by their descendants.

exogamy Contrasted with endogamy, the practice of marrying or mating "out."

false consciousness In Marxism and cultural materialism, the capability of people to misrepresent the meaning of their behaviour to themselves and to others.

father figures In Freudian psychology, totems that represent culturally ambivalent attitudes toward adult men.

female infanticide The practice of treating male children more favourably than female children, resulting in more female deaths.

fields A concept formulated by French sociologist Pierre Bourdieu to describe the ever-dynamic configuration, or network, of objective relationship between social agents and positions.

fixed action pattern An analytical construct of human ethology. See innate releasing mechanism and key stimulus.

folk taxonomies In cognitive anthropology, culturally conditioned "maps" of a semantic domain.

formalists Contrasted with substantivists, economic anthropologists who maintained that Western economic concepts apply to non-Western economies.

French rationalism The intellectual tradition associated with René Descartes and the scientific epistemology of deduction.

French structural anthropology The theoretical orientation of Claude Lévi-Strauss and his followers, involving elementary structures, reciprocity, and binary oppositions.

Freudian anthropology Also called psychodynamic anthropology, the school of psychological anthropology that adopted certain elements of Freudian psychology.

functionalism In British social anthropology, Alfred Reginald Radcliffe-Brown's theory of how parts of society contribute to the whole of society, sometimes called social physiology; *and* Bronislaw Malinowski's theory of how culture responds to biological needs in a hierarchically organized way.

functionalist archaeology Archaeology done in conjunction with functionalism.

geisteswissenschaften Translated "human sciences." Contrast with *naturwissenschaften*.

genealogical method Fieldwork that focuses on kinship.

generalized exchange According to Claude Lévi-Strauss, the exchange of women among more than two kinship groups, promoting greater social solidarity than restricted exchange.

general systems theory A cybernetic model for culture used in the New Archaeology.

gestalt A psychological configuration, in psychological anthropology sometimes attributed to a whole culture.

Great Chain of Being An influential medieval philosophical schema that ranked all cosmic elements lineally and hierarchically.

great man theory of history The theory that individuals affect the course of history more than do historical circumstances.

group mind Sometimes called collective consciousness, in Durkheimian social theory the source of collective representations or social facts.

group selection A vision of natural selection in which individuals behave altruistically, helping their group and thereby helping themselves. Contrast with kin selection.

habitus A term used by French social theorist Pierre Bourdieu to describe the capacity of individuals to innovate social and cultural form, based on their personal histories and social positioning within a community.

hegemony In the social sciences, a term referring to the capacity of one social group to impose particular beliefs or political and economic conditions upon another group.

heliocentrism Literally "sun-centredness," the view in diffusionism that world civilization arose around a cultural complex of sun worship in Egypt, then spread elsewhere.

historical particularism The anthropological orientation of Franz Boas and many of his students, focusing on the particular histories of cultures.

holistic "Well-rounded," overarching or broad.

human biogram A term used in human ethology to describe the alleged suite of inherited predispositions of *Homo sapiens*.

human ethology A hereditarian approach to the study of human behaviour derived in part from Darwinism and employing the analytical constructs of fixed action pattern, innate releasing mechanism, and key stimulus.

hypothetico-deductive model A philosophical model for scientific explanation used in the New Archaeology.

hysteria The psychological condition that got Sigmund Freud interested in psychology.

id Or libido, according to Sigmund Freud, the part of the psyche that expresses natural desire.

idealistic Pertaining to idealism, a general perspective in the social sciences that looks to systems of ideas and meanings, as opposed to the material conditions of existence, as the wellspring of human society and culture. See idealists and materialism.

idealists According to cultural materialism, followers of cultural idealism, the belief that, more often than not, changes occur first in emic superstructure, reverberate through etic superstructure and structure, and affect etic infrastructure last. Contrast with infrastructural determinism and eclectics.

ideology A term employed extensively by Karl Marx and scholars working in the tradition of Marxism to denote a system of beliefs that knowingly or unknowingly influences the perspectives and outlooks of individuals and groups.

idiographic Particularizing. Contrast with nomothetic.

The Imperial Synthesis Nineteenth-century archaeology linked to racism and colonialism.

incest Culturally proscribed inbreeding, according to Sigmund Freud an act that led to the primal patricide.

inclusive fitness In sociobiology, the measure, or result, of kin selection.

independent invention The nineteenth-century doctrine, linked to psychic unity, that a cultural innovation can occur in more than one place independently. Contrast with diffusionism.

indirect rule The British colonial policy of cooperating with native leaders in an attempt to avoid having to govern by force.

induction In scientific epistemology, the process of arriving at generalizations about particular facts. Contrast with deduction.

informant In anthropological fieldwork, someone who provides information.

infrastructural determinism In cultural materialism, the name for the belief that, more often than not, changes occur first in etic infrastructure, reverberate through etic structure and superstructure, and affect emic superstructure last. See eclectics.

inheritance of acquired characteristics The primary mechanism of evolution proposed by Jean Lamarck. Contrast with natural selection.

innate releasing mechanism An analytical construct of human ethnology. See fixed action pattern and key stimulus.

inner-worldly asceticism In Max Weber's scheme of cultural evolution, referring to the ethical demand of Protestant Calvinism that Christians not retreat from the world in order to live lives of piety, simplicity, and self-denial.

interpretive anthropology The anthropological school, associated with Clifford Geertz, espousing the view that culture is lived experience integrated in a coherent, public system of symbols that renders the world intelligible.

invented tradition A phrase describing the modern invention of historical events and personages, often with the goal of legitimizing contemporary political or religious ideologies by linking them directly to Antiquity.

key stimulus An analytical construct of human ethology. See fixed action pattern and innate releasing mechanism.

kinesics The scientific study of human body motion. See body language and proxemics.

kin selection In sociobiology, the principle that attempts to explain altruism by showing that altruists are really selfish, sometimes called the biology of nepotism. See group selection and natural selection.

kulturkreis Translated "culture circle," a concept central to some versions of diffusionism.

labour theory of value The Marxist proposition that commodities should be valued in terms of the human labour required to produce them.

Lamarckism A loosely used term referring to the evolutionism of Jean Lamarck, especially his mechanism of the inheritance of acquired characteristics.

law of universal gravitation Isaac Newton's scientific explanation of universal motion.

layer cake model of culture Leslie White's model of culture, with technology and economy at the bottom, ideology at the top, and social and political organization in between.

liminal An ephemeral psychosocial "space" in which social roles and arrangements are subject to transformation, inversion, and affirmation. See symbolic anthropology.

maintenance systems In the psychological anthropological model of John Whiting and Irvin Child, the equivalent of Abram Kardiner's primary cultural institutions without Freudian components.

Marxism A loosely used term referring to various views derived from Karl Marx and Friedrich Engels and dialectical materialism.

Marxist archaeology Archaeology done in conjunction with Marxism.

materialism In dialectical materialism, the belief that human existence determines human consciousness; in cultural materialism, the equivalent of the principle of infrastructural determinism.

matrilateral cross-cousin marriage Marriage of ego to a child of mother's brother. Contrast with patrilateral cross-cousin marriage.

matrilineal Unilineal kinship systems reckoned through the female line.

means of production In dialectical materialism, how people make a living in the material world.

mechanical philosophy The philosophy inspired by the law of universal gravitation, portraying the universe as a complex machine with fine-tuned, interacting parts.

mechanical solidarity According to Émile Durkheim, social cohesion maintained by individuals' similarities. Contrast with organic solidarity.

mechanics The medieval science of motion.

medical anthropology The cross-cultural, pan-historical study of sickness and health.

Midwestern Taxonomic Method The archaeological classification used in culture-historical archaeology.

missing links Perceived gaps in the evolutionary record.

monogenesis The doctrine that human races constitute a single species with a common origin and differences produced over time. Contrast with polygenesis.

monotheism Contrasted with polytheism, the belief in a single deity.

Moundbuilder Myth The myth that a mysterious people, not Indians, built impressive earthen mounds throughout the American Midwest.

multilineal Max Weber's view of cultural change and development as occurring in fits and starts, according to different social and historical contexts; *and* Julian Steward's name for his version of cultural neo-evolutionism contrasted with the universal version of Leslie White and the unilineal version of classical cultural evolutionism.

naked apery A disparaging term used to describe unfounded assertions about the inheritance of human behaviour.

national character A focus of psychological anthropology in the era of the Second World War.

natural children A theological modification of the conception of natural slaves allowing non-Europeans to improve themselves and convert to Christianity.

natural selection Charles Darwin's primary mechanism for biological evolution, involving struggle for existence and survival of the fittest. Contrast with inheritance of acquired characteristics.

natural slaves An early European conception of non-Europeans as innately imperfect and subservient. See natural children.

naturwissenschaften Translated "natural sciences." Contrast with *geisteswissenschaften*.

neo-evolutionists Twentieth-century anthropologists who revived and reformulated classical cultural evolutionism.

Neolithic Or New Stone Age, the period of prehistory characterized by polished stone tools and the domestication of animals and plants.

Neptunists Geologists who proposed that major geological changes were caused by the subsidence of water. Contrast with Vulcanists.

New Archaeology The nomothetic archaeology advocated by Lewis

Binford and others, also called processual archeology.

New Ethnography A term used to describe cognitive anthropology when the methodologies of ethnoscience and ethnolinguistics were in fact new.

New Physical Anthropology The name for physical anthropology committed to the synthetic theory of evolution.

New Stone Age Or Neolithic, the period of prehistory characterized by polished stone tools and the domestication of animals and plants.

noble savagery Romanticizing primitive life.

nomothetic Generalizing. Contrast with idiographic.

Oedipus complex According to Sigmund Freud, the troublesome psychological state of boys induced by their sexual desire for their mothers. Contrast with Electra complex.

Old Stone Age Or Paleolithic, the period of prehistory characterized by chipped and flaked stone tools and hunting and gathering subsistence.

ontogeny The growth of an individual. See phylogeny and biogenetic law.

organic solidarity According to Émile Durkheim, social cohesion maintained by individuals' differences. Contrast with mechanical solidarity.

organismic analogy Portraying society as an organism, as in social morphology and social physiology.

original sin The Christian idea that early sin resulted in the expulsion of humanity from the Garden of Eden.

orthogenesis The idea that biological evolution operates in one direction, usually in the direction of *Homo sapiens*.

Paleolithic Or Old Stone Age, the period of prehistory characterized by chipped and flaked stone tools and subsistence by hunting and gathering.

paradigms According to historian and philosopher of science Thomas Kuhn, intellectual frameworks for "normal" science that are superseded by scientific "revolutions."

participant-observation The anthropological style of fieldwork that requires the fieldworker to see things from the native point of view and at the same time remain objective.

patrilateral cross-cousin marriage Marriage of ego to a child of father's sister. Contrast with matrilateral cross-cousin marriage.

patrilineal Unilineal kinship systems reckoned through the male line.

personality variables In the psychological anthropological model of John Whiting and Irvin Child, the equivalent of Abram Kardiner's basic personality structure without Freudian components.

phenotype The product of gene action, often affected by environment. See behavioural genetics and polygenic.

philosophical anarchist One who, following philosopher Paul Feyerband, believes that all scientific paradigms are logically equivalent and therefore that there is no logical way to choose among them.

phonemes Minimally contrasting pairs of sounds that create linguistic meaning. See phonemics.

phonemics The study of linguistic meaning. See emic.

phonetics The study of linguistic sounds. See etic.

phylogeny The evolutionary growth of a species. See ontogeny and biogenetic law.

pietistic Petaining to piety, or religious reverence and devotion.

pleasure principle According to Sigmund Freud, the practice of acting libidinously, directed by the id. See reality principle.

political economy An anthropological perspective that came to prominence in the 1970s viewing sociocultural form at the local level as penetrated and influenced by global capitalism.

polyandry Mating or marriage involving one woman and more than one man.

polygenic Variation in phenotype affected by the action of many genes. See behavioural genetics.

polygenesis The doctrine that human races constitute multiple species with separate origins and innate differences. Contrast with monogenesis.

polytheism Contrasted with monotheism, the belief in multiple deities.

positivism The philosophy of science. See critical anthropologists.

Positivism The scientific philosophy of Auguste Comte.

postmodernism A general movement within the social sciences and humanities that during the 1980s and 1990s sought to question the possibility of impartiality, objectivity or authoritative knowledge.

post-processualists Archaeologists critical of nomothetic New

Archaeology, also called **contextual** archaeologists.

poststructural In anthropology, an adjective that expresses disenchantment with static, mechanistic, and controlling models of society and culture and a consequent interest in social process and **agency**.

potlatch A North American Indian ceremonial feast analyzed in diverse ways by anthropologists.

practice Or **praxis**, a concept pioneered by French social theorist Pierre Bourdieu holding that society and culture are constructed by purposeful, creative agents who bring to life their society and culture through talk and action, making their creations appear to be objective facts of nature rather than arbitrary constructs imagined and assembled by people.

Prague School A school of linguists who pioneered analysis of the phoneme and influenced **French structural anthropology**.

praxis See **practice**.

prehistory The period of human existence before writing.

primal patricide In Sigmund Freud's reconstructed **primeval family**, the killing of the father by his sons, an act of profound consequence.

primary cultural institutions In **psychodynamic** anthropology, institutions that affect how children are raised and shape **basic personality structure**.

primeval family In Sigmund Freud's reconstruction of human history, the first family form — monogamous, nuclear, and patriarchal.

primitive communism In some versions of **Marxism**, the view that past primitive peoples lived in a state to which future communism will, in a fashion, return.

processual archaeology According to post-processualists, nomothetic New Archaeology.

profane In the writings of Émile Durkheim, the profane refers to that which is routine, mundane, impure, and "of the world." This contrasts with the sacred, which is pure and transcends everyday experience.

projective systems In the psychological anthropological model of John Whiting and Irvin Child, the equivalent of Abram Kardiner's secondary cultural institutions without Freudian components.

proletariat In Marxism, the working class.

proxemics The scientific study of body positioning. See body language and kinesics.

psyche According to Sigmund Freud, the subconscious, comprising the id, ego, and superego.

psychic unity The doctrine that all peoples have the same fundamental capacity for change.

psychodynamic The school of psychological anthropology that adopted certain elements of Freudian psychology, often called Freudian anthropology.

psychological anthropology Anthropology concerned with the relationship between cultures and personalities.

racial memory According to Sigmund Freud, our subconscious awareness of the history of the human psyche.

rationalized According to Max Weber, evolved through the progressive systematization of ideas, the subsequent establishment of norms of behaviours in accordance with those ideas, and a motivational commitment to such norms.

reality principle According to Sigmund Freud, the principle of realizing that acting on the pleasure principle is dangerous and immature.

reciprocal altruism In sociobiology, a mechanism said to account for altruism among non-relatives.

reciprocity For Marcel Mauss, the elementary principle of exchanging gifts; for Claude Lévi-Strauss and French structural anthropology, the elementary principle of exchanging women.

relatively non-privileged A phrase coined by Max Weber to describe those socioeconomic classes most prone to the creation of new social forms in complex or differentiated societies.

religion An integrated system of meanings and practices that seeks to connect humankind with a divine or metaphysical order, whether this connection manifests itself in ritual propitiation (i.e., worship), control (i.e., magic) or some combination of the two.

restricted exchange According to Claude Lévi-Strauss, the exchange of women between two kinship groups, promoting less social solidarity than generalized exchange.

revitalization movement A term coined by Anthony F. C. Wallace to describe the spontaneous evolution of culture that occurs when communities experience conditions of extreme social and economic duress or marginalization.

ritual Any form of prescribed behaviour that is periodically repeated, and that links the actions of the individual or group to a metaphysical order of existence.

ruling class In dialectical materialism, the class that controls the means of production.

sacred In the writings of Émile Durkheim, the sacred refers to that which is pure, powerful, and supernatural, and must therefore be set apart from the routine, the mundane, and the worldly. The inverse of profane.

salvage ethnography Ethnography motivated by the need to obtain information about cultures threatened with extinction or assimilation.

salvation In Max Weber's usage, escape from the world's capriciousness and evil through social arrangements rationalized in accordance with a divine plan, typically revealed by charismatic prophets.

Sapir-Whorf hypothesis The proposition that the structure of language and the structure of thought correspond, with the structure of language preponderant.

savagery, barbarism, and civilization A tripartite chronological schema popular in classical cultural evolutionism.

scientific racism According to its critics, improper or incorrect science that promotes or supports racism.

secondary cultural institutions In psychodynamic anthropology, institutions that are projections of basic personality structure and help people cope with the world.

second law of thermodynamics In thermodynamics, the proposition that the universe is running down and generating increased entropy.

semantic domain A culturally meaningful mental domain, the focus of inquiry in cognitive anthropology.

semiotic Pertaining to the relationship between symbols and what they represent. See symbolic anthropology.

seriationally According to the archaeological principle of seriation, or relative dating by the evolution of artifact style.

sexual selection Charles Darwin's mechanism for human evolution, used in sociobiology to explain differences between males and females.

shamans Magico-religious specialists who communicate with ancestral ghosts and souls.

social constructionism A contemporary anthropological theory holding that all sociocultural phenomena are products of historically-situated interpersonal "negotiation," as accomplished through patterned language and activity.

Social Darwinism A loosely used term referring to social philosophies based on Darwinian evolutionism, especially the mechanism of natural selection.

social dynamics In Positivism, the study of social change.

social facts Émile Durkheim's name for social phenomena, his units of sociological analysis.

social function In British social anthropology, the contribution of a part of society to the whole of society, sometimes called social physiology.

social morphology In British social anthropology, according to the organismic analogy, the study of social structure.

social physiology In British social anthropology, according to the organismic analogy, the study of social function.

social statics In Positivism, the study of social stability.

social structure In British social anthropology, the social matrix of behaviour, sometimes called social morphology.

sociobiology An investigation of the biological basis of social behaviour using the evolutionary principles of kin selection and inclusive fitness.

solipsism The idea that the individual self is the only reality, and that the whole external world exists only in one's imagination, or dreamstate.

Southwest School A group of philosophers from whom Franz Boas learned to differentiate human and natural sciences. See *naturwissenschaften* and *geisteswissenschaften*.

species A group of organisms whose members can reproduce only with one another.

status societies In the schema of Henry Maine, societies that were family-oriented, held property in common, and maintained control by social sanctions, contrasted with contract societies.

Stone Age The Old Stone Age, or Paleolithic, and the New Stone Age, or Neolithic.

stratigraphy The archaeological dating of artifacts relative to their placement in systematically layered earth.

structural-functionalism In British social anthropology, the synchronic concern with social structure and social function.

structuralism In British social anthropology, the synchronic concern with social structure, the social matrix of behaviour, sometimes called social morphology; in French structural anthropology, the concern with elementary forms of minds and cultures.

structural Marxists Proponents of structural Marxism, a theoretical blend of Marxism, dialectical philosophy, and French structural anthropology.

struggle for existence Charles Darwin's view that evolution involves competition for limited resources, resulting in survival of the fittest. See natural selection.

subconscious According to Sigmund Freud, a part of our minds of which we are only unconsciously aware, seat of our psyche.

sublimate According to Sigmund Freud, to rechannel libidinous desires into culturally acceptable thoughts and behaviours.

substantivists Contrasted with formalists, economic anthropologists who maintained that Western economic concepts do not apply to non-Western economies.

superego According to Sigmund Freud, the part of the psyche that monitors the id and mediates between the ego and the outside world, sometimes called conscience.

superorganic The idea that culture is distinct from and "above" biology.

survival of the fittest In Darwinian evolution, the outcome of the struggle for existence, resulting in adaptation. See natural selection.

survivals Edward Burnett Tylor's name for nonfunctional cultural traits that are clues to the past.

swamping effect In Charles Darwin's time, the name given to the observation that small variations serving as raw material for natural selection would always be diluted through heredity.

symbolic anthropology The anthropological school, associated with Victor Turner, espousing the view that social solidarity is a function of the systems of symbolic logic that connect people, especially during ritual.

sympathetic magic Magic that can affect an object through a similar object.

synchronic Ahistorical, unconcerned with the past. Contrast with diachronic.

synthetic philosophy The all-encompassing philosophy of Herbert Spencer, based on the premise that homogeneity is evolving into heterogeneity everywhere.

synthetic theory of evolution The twentieth-century theoretical synthesis of Darwinian evolutionism and Mendelian genetics.

taboos Culturally sanctioned prohibitions.

tabula rasa Translated "blank slate," the idea that our minds acquire knowledge through experience rather than recognize knowledge that is innate.

teleology The idea that biological evolution adheres to a long-term purpose or goal.

text In the interpretive anthropology of Clifford Geertz, the equivalent of culture, interpreted through a process of thick description.

theistic Pertaining to theism, the view that God created the universe and remains active in its day-to-day operations. Contrast with deistic.

theodicy A term borrowed from Christian theology by Max Weber and used to describe the explanation, even justification, of evil in the world despite the existence of an omnipotent, just, and loving God.

thermodynamic law The nomothetic basis of Leslie White's culturology, symbolized $E \times T = C$.

thermodynamics The study of conversion of energy in the universe, a fundamental part of culturology as expressed in the second law of thermodynamics.

thesis-antithesis-synthesis In dialectical materialism, philosopher Friedrich Hegel's formulation of dialectical change.

thick description In the interpretive anthropology of Clifford Geertz, the process of interpreting culture as text.

Three Age System The archaeological ages of Stone, Bronze, and Iron.

totems Objects of collective cultural veneration. A term that Sigmund Freud employed to represent father figures, and that Émile Durkheim employed to refer to certain ritual objects that embody the sacred sentiments of a society, and so stimulate feelings of "effervescence" and of greater reality existing outside the individual.

transmigrate To pass into another body after death, as do spirits and ghosts.

typological thinking Failure to appreciate the significant variation that exists within biological populations, which was the key to Charles Darwin's theory of evolution by natural selection.

uniformitarianism Contrasted with catastrophism, the geological doctrine that present nondramatic agents of geological change have operated throughout the past.

unilineal Julian Steward's description of classical cultural evolutionism. Contrast with multilineal and universal.

unilineal kinship systems Kinship systems reckoned through one parental line, either matrilineal or patrilineal.

universal Julian Steward's description of the cultural neo-evolutionism of Leslie White. Contrast with multilineal and unilineal.

universal historians Enlightenment thinkers who promulgated laws of human history.

universal pattern In cultural materialism, the levels of culture — infrastructure, structure, and superstructure — with emic and etic and mental and behavioural dimensions.

variables Carefully defined units of analysis that can be manipulated statistically and yield correlations.

vitalism The idea that biological evolution is self-motivated or willed.

volksgeist Translated "spirit of the people," a sense of ethnic or racial distinctness that permeated some styles of ethnography, notably German.

Vulcanists Geologists who proposed that major geological changes were caused by the elevation of land brought about by subterranean heat. Contrast with Neptunists.

vulgar materialists A label for cultural materialists who, according to their critics, ignore dialectical thinking.

world-system A phrase used in political economy to describe the global expansion of Western capitalism, its penetration into and progressive homogenization of all societies, and its incorporation of those societies into an international system of unequal commodity exchange.

xenophobic Pertaining to xenophobia, the fear and dislike of "foreigners."

suggested further reading

This list of suggested further reading comprises citations of books culled from a vast literature in the history of anthropological theory. The list concentrates on secondary sources, or sources written *about* the past, but includes some primary sources, or sources written *in* the past (in a few instances near the present). A much lengthier list of citations of books, book chapters, monographs, articles, and dissertations can be found in *History of Anthropology Bibliography*, compiled by Paul A. Erickson (Toronto: Canadian Scholar's Press, 1997). Citations of publications also appear regularly in *History of Anthropology Newsletter*, edited by George W. Stocking, Jr., of the University of Chicago. Readers may wish to search the Internet for additional resources; a good place to begin is the site "Anthropological Resources on the World Wide Web" (http://server. berkeley.edu/AUA/resources.html).

If, at the time of writing, a book was in print, its latest published citation is provided. If a book was out of print, its citation is derived from another book or from the source itself. Although many books are relevant to more than one chapter, they are listed only once. Some original or earlier dates of publication appear in brackets [ ]. For certain reprint editions, dates appear in brackets only.

Anthropology in Antiquity

Cole, Thomas (1967) *Democritus and the Sources of Greek Anthropology.* Cleveland, Ohio: Western Reserve University Press.
A study of the roots of anthropology in Antiquity, emphasizing a Greek philosopher of materialism.

Darnell, Regna (Ed.) (1974) *Readings in the History of Anthropology*. New York: Harper and Row.
A collection of primary sources including some from ancient times.

Edelstein, Ludwig (1967) *The Idea of Progress in Classical Antiquity*. Baltimore: The Johns Hopkins University Press.
An examination of the ancient foundations of an idea linked to the history of anthropological theory.

Gernet, Louis [1981] *The Anthropology of Ancient Greece*. Ann Arbor, Michigan: Books on Demand.
A valuable historical study.

Humphreys, S.C. (1984) *Anthropology and the Greeks*. New York: Routledge.
A book of anthropology in and about Greece.

Kluckhohn, Clyde [1961] *Anthropology and the Classics*. Ann Arbor, Michigan: Books on Demand.
A study by a distinguished American anthropologist.

Malefijt, Annemarie de Waal (1977) *Images of Man: A History of Anthropological Thought*. New York: Alfred Knopf.
An intellectual and social history of anthropological theory beginning in classical times.

Snowden, Frank M., Jr. (1991) *Before Color Prejudice: The Ancient View of Blacks*. Cambridge, Massachusetts: Harvard University Press.
An historical study of the cultural contexts of race and racism.

Voget, Fred W. (1975) *A History of Ethnology*. New York: Holt, Rinehart and Winston.
A compendium of ethnological developments beginning in Antiquity.

The Middle Ages

Boas, George (1966) *Essays on Primitivism and Related Ideas in the Middle Ages.* New York: Octagon Books.
Analyses of ideas that have influenced — and, in turn, been influenced by — anthropology.

Brehaut, Ernest (1964) *An Encyclopedist of the Dark Ages, Isidore of Seville.* New York: B. Franklin.
A biographical account of the life and times of one of the most influential early Christian historians.

Friedman, John B. [1963] *The Monstrous Races in Medieval Art and Thought.* Ann Arbor, Michigan: Books on Demand.
An historical account of the anthropologically exotic.

Lovejoy, Arthur O. (1936) *Great Chain of Being: A Study of the History of an Idea.* Cambridge, Massachusetts: Harvard University Press.
An analysis of a philosophical schema that prevailed during the Middle Ages and shaped anthropology.

Mahdi, Muhsin (1957) *Ibn Khaldûn's Philosophy of History: A Study in the Philosophic Foundation of the Science of Culture.* London: G. Allen and Unwin.
An analysis of the work of a medieval Islamic historian who described Arab and Bedouin culture "scientifically."

The Renaissance

Allen, Don C. [1963] *The Legend of Noah: Renaissance Rationalism in Art, Science and Letters.* Ann Arbor, Michigan: Books on Demand.
An analysis of Renaissance thought that highlights Christianity.

Dudley, Edward J., and Maximillian E. Novak (Eds.) [1972] *The Wild Man Within: An Image in Western Thought from the Renaissance to Romanticism.* Ann Arbor, Michigan: Books on Demand.
The history of an image incorporated into many anthropological portrayals of non-Western peoples.

Levin, Harry (1969) *The Myth of the Golden Age in the Renaissance.* Bloomington: Indiana University Press.
An examination of the Renaissance discovery of Greco-Roman glories.

Penrose, Boies (1955) *Travel and Discovery in the Renaissance, 1420-1620.* Cambridge, Massachusetts: Harvard University Press.
An account of the early phases of European global exploration.

Piggott, Stuart (1989) *Ancient Britons and Antiquarian Imagination.* New York: Thames and Hudson.
A distinguished British archaeologist writes about the development of antiquarianism in the Renaissance.

Trigger, Bruce (1990) *A History of Archaeological Thought.* New York: Cambridge University Press.
A comprehensive history of archaeology beginning with classical Renaissance historicism.

Voyages of Geographical Discovery

Asad, Talal (Ed.) (1974) *Anthropology and the Colonial Encounter.* Atlantic Highlands, New Jersey: Humanities Press International.
A history of anthropology in the context of European colonialism.

Banton, Michael (1987) *Racial Theories.* New York: Cambridge University Press.
A history of racial theories as both cause and effect of interactions among human populations.

Berkhofer, Robert F., Jr. (1979) *The White Man's Indian: Images of the American Indian from Columbus to the Present*. New York: Random House.
A history of American Indians as seen through the eyes of "whites."

Bieder, Robert E. (1986) *Science Encounters the Indian, Eighteen Twenty to Eighteen Eighty: The Early Years of American Ethnology*. Norman: University of Oklahoma Press.
A history of early American ethnology shaped by interactions between aboriginal and non-aboriginal populations.

Campbell, Mary B. (1988) *The Witness and the Other World: Exotic European Travel Writing, 400-1600*. Ithaca, New York: Cornell University Press.
An examination of the early phase of European geographical exploration.

Cohen, William B. [1980] *The French Encounter with Africans: White Response to Blacks, 1530-1880*. Ann Arbor, Michigan: Books on Demand.
A history of French attitudes toward Africans in the early colonial period.

Curtin, Philip D. [1964] *The Image of Africa: British Ideas and Action, 1780-1850*. Ann Arbor, Michigan: Books on Demand.
A history of British attitudes toward Africans in the early colonial period.

Dickason, Olive Patricia (1984) *The Myth of the Savage and the Beginnings of French Colonialism in the Americas*. Edmonton: University of Alberta Press.
An account of how early French perceptions of aboriginal Americans influenced French colonialism.

Dussel, Enrique (1995) *The Invention of the Americas: Eclipse of "The Other" and the Myth of Modernity*. New York: Continuum.
An account of the origin of an anthropological image of America.

Garbarino, Merwyn S. (1983) *Sociocultural Theory in Anthropology: A Short History*. Prospect Heights, Illinois: Waveland Press.
A concise history of major sociocultural theories beginning with the period of European geographical exploration.

Hammond, Dorothy, and Alta Jablow [1992] *The Africa that Never Was: Four Centuries of British Writing about Africa — An Anthropological View Contrasting the Africa of Fact and the Africa of Fiction.* Rev. ed. Prospect Heights, Illinois: Waveland Press.
A revisionist history of the British depiction of Africa.

Hanzeli, Victor E. (1969) *Missionary Linguistics in New France: A Study of Seventeenth and Eighteenth Century Descriptions of American Indian Languages.* The Hague: Mouton.
An assessment of the linguistic writings of early French missionaries in America.

Hodgen, Margaret T. (1964) *Early Anthropology in the Sixteenth and Seventeenth Centuries.* Philadelphia: University of Pennsylvania Press.
Accounts of anthropology in the early modern period.

Huddleston, Lee Eldridge (1967) *Origins of American Indians: European Concepts, 1492-1729.* Austin: University of Texas Press.
A history of early European attempts to explain the origin of American Indians.

Moore, Sally Falk (1994) *Anthropology and Africa: Changing Perspectives on a Changing Scene.* Charlottesville: University Press of Virginia.
An account of how changes in Africa have interacted with changing anthropological views of Africa.

Pagden, Anthony (1987) *The Fall of Natural Man: The American Indian and the Origins of Comparative Ethnology.* New York: Cambridge University Press.
An account of how Europeans' early perceptions of American Indians affected both populations.

Schwartz, Stuart B. (Ed.) (1994) *Implicit Understandings: Observing, Reporting and Reflecting on the Encounters Between Europeans and Other Peoples in the Early Modern Era.* New York: Cambridge University Press.
Analyses of early encounters between Europeans and non-Europeans.

Stocking, George W., Jr. (Ed.) (1993) *Colonial Situations: Essays on the Contextualization of Ethnographic Knowledge.* Madison: University of Wisconsin Press.
Analyses of anthropology in the context of colonialism.

Wauchope, Robert [1962] *Lost Tribes and Sunken Continents: Myth and Method in the Study of American Indians.* Ann Arbor, Michigan: Books on Demand.
An account of early theories linking American Indians to Europeans.

The Scientific Revolution

Hall, Marie Boas (1962) *Scientific Renaissance, 1450-1630.* New York: Harper.
A history of key developments in the Scientific Revolution.

Henry, John (1997) *The Scientific Revolution and the Origins of Modern Science.* Old Tappan, New Jersey: Macmillan.
A concise history of the Scientific Revolution.

Hull, David (1990) *Science as Process: An Evolutionary Account of the Social and Conceptual Development of Science.* Chicago: University of Chicago Press.
An account of how science develops in social contexts.

Kuhn, Thomas S. (1970) *The Structure of Scientific Revolutions.* 2nd ed. Chicago: University of Chicago Press.
An influential history of the Scientific Revolution as a shift of paradigms.

The Enlightenment

Bryson, Gladys (1968) [1945] *Man and Society: The Scottish Enlightenment of the Eighteenth Century.* New York: Augustus M. Kelly.
An examination of Scottish Enlightenment contributions to anthropology.

Cloyd, E. L. (1972) *James Burnett, Lord Monboddo*. Oxford: Clarendon Press.
A biography of an Enlightenment thinker who thought that a properly conditioned ape could learn to talk like a human being.

Daiches, David, Peter Jones, and Jean Jones (Eds.) (1986) *A Hotbed of Genius: The Scottish Enlightenment, 1730-1790*. Edinburgh: Edinburgh University Press.
An intellectual history of the Scottish Enlightenment.

Danesi, Marcel (Ed.) (1995) *Giambattista Vico and Anglo-American Science: Philosophy and Writing*. Berlin: Mouton de Gruyter.
An assessment of the contributions of the influential Italian Enlightenment thinker.

Harris, Marvin (1968) *The Rise of Anthropological Theory: A History of Theories of Culture*. New York: Harper Collins.
Theories of culture critiqued from the perspective of cultural materialism, beginning with the Enlightenment.

Jones, Peter (Ed.) (1991) *The Science of Man in the Scottish Enlightenment: Hume, Reid and their Contemporaries*. New York: Columbia University Press.
Assessments of the anthropological relevance of key Scottish Enlightenment figures.

Locke, John (1994) [1690] *An Essay Concerning Human Understanding*. Amherst, New York: Prometheus Books.
An essay setting forth Locke's concept of *tabula rasa*, an intellectual foundation of the Enlightenment.

Mali, Joseph (1992) *The Rehabilitation of Myth: Vico's New Science*. New York: Cambridge University Press.
An appraisal of the work of Giambattista Vico.

Miller, Cecilia (1993) *Giambattista Vico: Imagination and Historical Knowledge.* New York: St. Martin's Press.
Another account of Vico's life and times.

Rousseau, George Sebastian, and Roy Porter (Eds.) (1990) *Exoticism in the Enlightenment.* Manchester: Manchester University Press.
European conceptualizations of "exotic-looking" peoples.

Saiedi, Nader (1992) *The Birth of Social Theory: Social Thought in the Enlightenment and Romanticism.* Lanham, Maryland: University Press of America.
The origins of social theory in the eighteenth and early nineteenth centuries.

The Rise of Positivism

Comte, Auguste [1830-1842] *Positive Philosophy.* Harriet Martineau, trans. New York: AMS Press.
August Comte's explication of Positivism.

Pickering, Mary (1993) *Auguste Comte: An Intellectual Biography, Vol. I.* New York: Cambridge University Press.
A partial intellectual biography of the architect of nineteenth-century positivist philosophy.

Marxism

Archibald, W. Peter (1992) *Marx and the Missing Link: Human Nature.* Atlantic Highlands, New Jersey: Humanities Press International.
An evaluation of Karl Marx' anthropological thinking.

Berlin, Isaiah (1996) *Karl Marx: His Life and Environment.* 4th ed. New York: Oxford University Press.
A biographical account of the life and times of Karl Marx.

Engels, Friedrich (1972) [1884] *Origin of the Family, Private Property, and the State*. 2nd ed. Eleanor B. Leacock, ed. New York: International Publishers Company.
Engels' views on cultural evolution.

Marx, Karl, and Friedrich Engels (1992) [1848] *The Communist Manifesto*. David McLellan, ed. New York: Oxford University Press.
Marx' and Engels' exposition of dialectical materialism.

Woolfson, Charles (1982) *The Labour Theory of Culture: A Re-Examination of Engels' Theory of Human Origins*. London: Routledge.
An evaluation of Friedrich Engels' writings on anthropology.

Classical Cultural Evolutionism

Ackerman, Robert (1990) *J. G. Frazer: His Life and Work*. New York: Cambridge University Press.
A biography of the classical cultural evolutionist who studied myth, folklore, and religion.

Bowler, Peter J. (1990) *The Invention of Progress: The Victorians and the Past*. Cambridge, Massachusetts: Blackwell.
An examination of the relationship between the ideas of progress and the past in Victorian times.

Burrow, J. W. (1966) *Evolution and Society: A Study in Victorian Social Theory*. London: Cambridge University Press.
A study of evolutionism as an expression of Victorian themes.

Coombes, Annie E. (1994) *Reinventing Africa: Museums, Material Culture, and Popular Imagination in Late Victorian and Edwardian England*. New Haven, Connecticut: Yale University Press.
An evaluation of the role of museums in shaping and reflecting European attitudes toward Africans.

Diamond, Alan (Ed.) (1991) *The Victorian Achievement of Sir Henry Maine: A Centennial Appraisal*. New York: Cambridge University Press.
Assessments of the lesser-known British classical cultural evolutionist.

Fortes, Meyer (1970) *Kinship and the Social Order: The Legacy of Lewis Henry Morgan*. Chicago: Aldine.
Evaluation of a nineteenth-century American cultural evolutionist by a twentieth-century British social anthropologist.

Frasen, Robert (1990) *The Making of The Golden Bough: The Origins and Growth of an Argument*. New York: St. Martin's Press.
A book about the evolution of James Frazer's *magnum opus*.

Frazer, James G. (1985) [1890] *The Golden Bough*. Abr. and rev. ed. Old Tappan, New Jersey: Macmillan.
An abbreviated version of Frazer's monumental multivolume work on the evolution of myth, folklore, and religion.

Hinsley, Curtis M., Jr. (1994) *The Smithsonian and the American Indian: Making a Moral Anthropology in Victorian America*. Washington, D.C.: Smithsonian Institution Press.
A study of the role a leading museum played in the development of nineteenth-century American anthropology.

Judd, Neil Merton (1967) *The Bureau of American Ethnology: A Partial History*. Norman: University of Oklahoma Press.
A history of one of the most influential institutions of anthropology in the United States.

Moore, Jerry D. (1997) *Visions of Culture: An Introduction to Anthropological Theories and Theorists*. Walnut Creek, California: Altimira Press.
Introductions to numerous influential cultural theorists, including some from the nineteenth century.

Morgan, Lewis Henry (1985) [1877] *Ancient Society*. Tucson: University of Arizona Press.
Morgan's *magnum opus*.

Rumney, Jay (1966) *Herbert Spencer's Sociology: A Study in the History of Social Theory*. New York: Atherton Press.
An account of Spencer as a social evolutionist.

Sanderson, Stephen K. (1992) *Social Evolutionism: A Critical History*. Cambridge, Massachusetts: Blackwell.
A critique of social evolutionism encompassing the Victorian era.

Spencer, Herbert [1967] *The Evolution of Society: Selections from Herbert Spencer's Principles of Sociology*. Robert L. Carneiro, ed. Ann Arbor, Michigan: Books on Demand.
A collection of Spencer's writings on social evolution.

Stocking, George W., Jr. (1987) *Victorian Anthropology*. New York: The Free Press.
A masterful history of anthropology in the Victorian era.

Stocking, George W., Jr. (1994) *The Collected Works of E. B. Tylor*. New York: Routledge.
A compendium of the writings of the Victorian "father" of British anthropology.

Stocking, George W., Jr. (Ed.) (1988) *Objects and Others: Essays on Museums and Material Culture*. Madison: University of Wisconsin Press.
A collection of writings on the roles of museums in anthropology.

Trautman, Robert R. (1987) *Lewis Henry Morgan and the Invention of Kinship*. Berkeley: University of California Press.
A biography of Morgan that places him on the foundation of the anthropological study of kinship.

Tylor, Edward Burnett (1873) [1871] *Primitive Culture*. New York: Gordon Press.
Tylor's summation of anthropological knowledge.

Tylor, Edward Burnett (1898) [1881] *Anthropology: An Introduction to the Study of Man and Civilization*. New York: D. Appleton.
The first anthropology "textbook."

Evolutionism vs. Diffusionism

Elkin, A.P., and N.W.G. Macintosh (Eds.) (1974) *Grafton Elliot Smith: The Man and His Work*. Sydney: Sydney University Press.
A collection of articles about a pioneering Australian anthropologist who espoused diffusionism.

Perry, William J. (1968) [1923] *Children of the Sun: A Study in the Early History of Civilization*. Saint Clair Shores, Michigan: Scholarly Press.
The book that explains why Perry believed civilization arose in Egypt and then spread elsewhere.

Archaeology Comes of Age

Bowden, Mark (1991) *Pitt Rivers: The Life and Archaeological Work of Lieutenant-General Augustus Henry Lane Fox Pitt Rivers, DCL, FRS, FSA*. New York: Cambridge University Press.
An intellectual biography of a pioneering British archaeologist.

Brunhouse, Robert Levere (1974) *In Search of the Maya: The First Archaeologists*. New York: Ballantine Books.
A lively account of the excitement surrounding early Mayan archaeology.

Claassen, Cheryl (Ed.) (1994) *Women in Archaeology*. Philadelphia: University of Pennsylvania Press.
A collection of articles by and about women archaeologists.

Daniel, Glyn E. (Ed.) (1981) *Towards a History of Archaeology*. New York: Thames and Hudson.

A collection of essays on the history of archaeology edited by a distinguished British prehistorian.

Daniel, Glyn E., and Colin Renfrew (1988) *The Idea of Prehistory*. 2nd ed. Edinburgh: Edinburgh University Press.

An account of developments leading to acceptance of the idea of prehistory in nineteenth-century Europe.

Drower, Margaret S. (1995) *Flinders Petrie: A Life in Archaeology*. Madison: University of Wisconsin Press.

A biography of the famous Egyptologist.

Givens, Douglas (1992) *Alfred Vincent Kidder and the Development of Americanist Archaeology*. Albuquerque: University of New Mexico Press.

A biography of a well-known early archaeologist of the American Southwest.

Gräslund, Bo (1987) *The Birth of Prehistoric Chronology: Dating Methods and Dating Systems in Nineteenth Century Scandinavian Archaeology*. New York: Cambridge University Press.

A history of archaeological dating techniques and chronologies, including the chronology of Three Ages.

Grayson, Donald K. (Ed.) (1983) *The Establishment of Human Antiquity*. Orlando, Florida: Academic Press.

Perspectives on the origins of the idea of human antiquity in nineteenth-century anthropology.

Hawkes, Jacquetta Hopkins (1982) *Adventurer in Archaeology: The Biography of Sir Mortimer Wheeler*. New York: St. Martin's Press.

A biography of one of the best known and most colourful twentieth-century British archaeologists.

Lubbock, John (1977) [1865] *Pre-Historic Times*. North Stratford, New Hampshire: Ayer.

Lubbock's summation of mid-nineteenth-century prehistoric archaeology.

Lyell, Charles [1863] *Geological Evidence of the Antiquity of Man*. 4th ed. New York: AMS Press.

Lyell's landmark summation of the evidence for human prehistoric antiquity.

Robertshaw, Peter (Ed.) (1990) *A History of African Archaeology*. Portsmouth, New Hampshire: Heinemann.

A collection of perspectives on the history of archaeology in the formerly colonized continent.

Rupke, Nicholas A. (1983) *The Great Chain of History: William Buckland and the English School of Geology (1814-1849)*. Oxford: Clarendon.

A history of the early exploration of British caves with prehistoric human remains.

Silverberg, Robert (1986) *The Mound-Builders*. Athens, Ohio: Ohio University Press.

A history of the myth that mysterious people, not Indians, built prehistoric earthen mounds throughout the Midwestern United States.

Squier, Ephraim G., and E.H. Davis [1848] *Ancient Monuments of the Mississippi Valley*. New York: AMS Press.

The landmark evaluation of evidence for prehistoric Mississippi Valley mound builders.

Van Riper, A. Bowdin (1993) *Men Among the Mammoths: Victorian Science and the Discovery of Human Prehistory*. Chicago: University of Chicago Press.

A detailed history of scientific developments in the 1850s and 1860s leading to acceptance of the idea of prehistory in Britain.

Willey, Gordon R., and Jeremy A. Sabloff (1995) *A History of American Archaeology*. 3rd ed. New York: W.H. Freeman.

A comprehensive history of American archaeology.

Darwinism

Bannister, Robert C. (1988) *Social Darwinism: Science and Myth*. Rev. ed. Philadelphia: Temple University Press.
An analysis of scientific and extrascientific rationalizations for a Darwinian interpretation of society.

Bowler, Peter J. (1983) *The Eclipse of Darwinism: Anti-Darwinian Evolution Theories in the Decades Around 1900*. Baltimore: Johns Hopkins University Press.
An explanation of how Darwin's theory of evolution by natural selection fell out of scientific favour by 1900.

Bowler, Peter J. (1986) *Theories of Human Evolution: A Century of Debate, 1844-1944*. Baltimore: Johns Hopkins University Press.
A history of ideas about human evolution in the pre- and post-Darwinian periods.

Bowler, Peter J. (1989) *Evolution: The History of an Idea*. Rev. ed. Berkeley: University of California Press.
A complex history of the idea of evolution.

Bowler, Peter J. (1989) *The Mendelian Revolution: The Emergence of Hereditarian Concepts in Modern Science and Society*. Baltimore: Johns Hopkins University Press.
An examination of "nature versus nurture" in the nineteenth and twentieth centuries.

Bowler, Peter J. (1996) *Charles Darwin: The Man and His Influence*. New York: Cambridge University Press.
A scientific biography of Darwin.

Burckhardt, Richard W., Jr. (1990) *The Spirit of System: Lamarck and Evolutionary Biology*. Cambridge, Massachusetts: Harvard University Press.
A scientific biography of the famous pre-Darwinian evolutionist Jean Lamarck.

Clements, Harry (1983) *Alfred Russel Wallace: Biologist and Social Reformer.* London: Hutchinson.
A biography of the co-discoverer of the idea of natural selection.

Darwin, Charles (1964) [1859] *On the Origin of Species: A Facsimile of the First Edition.* Cambridge, Massachusetts: Harvard University Press.
Darwin's *magnum opus.*

Darwin, Charles (1981) [1871] *The Descent of Man and Selection in Relation to Sex.* Princeton, New Jersey: Princeton University Press.
Darwin's explanation of human evolution.

Degler, Carl (1992) *In Search of Human Nature: The Decline and Revival of Darwinism in American Social Thought.* New York: Oxford University Press.
An examination of the ebb and flow of Social Darwinism in the United States.

Desmond, Adrian (1994) *Huxley: The Devil's Disciple.* London: Michael Joseph.
The first of a two-part biography of Darwin's "bulldog" Thomas Henry Huxley.

Desmond, Adrian (1997) *Huxley: Evolution's High Priest.* London: Michael Joseph.
The second of a two-part biography of Darwin's "bulldog" Thomas Henry Huxley.

Eckman, Paul (1973) *Darwin and Facial Expression: A Century of Research in Review.* Orlando, Florida: Academic Press.
A book that traces the history of human ethology back to Charles Darwin.

Eiseley, Loren C. (1958) *Darwin's Century: Evolution and the Men Who Discovered It.* Garden City, New York: Doubleday.
A non-technical history of key developments in Darwinism.

Gillispie, Charles C. (1996) [1951] *Genesis and Geology*. Cambridge, Massachusetts: Harvard University Press.
A study of the influence of Christian theology on geology in the decades leading up to *Origin of Species*.

Glick, Thomas F. (Ed.) (1988) *The Comparative Reception of Darwinism*. Chicago: University of Chicago Press.
A collection of articles examining the early reception of Darwinism in several countries.

Gould, Stephen Jay (1987) *Time's Arrow, Time's Cycle: Myth and Metaphor in the Discovery of Geological Time*. Cambridge, Massachusetts: Harvard University Press.
A book about influences on the geological conceptualization of time in the nineteenth century.

Gould, Stephen Jay (1996) *The Mismeasure of Man*. New York: W.W. Norton.
An examination of the use and abuse of anthropometric measurements by nineteenth-century racial anthropologists.

Greene, John C. (1959) *The Death of Adam: Evolution and its Impact on Western Thought*. Ames: Iowa State University Press.
An eloquent history of Darwinism and its implication for anthropology.

Haller, John S., Jr. (1995) [1971] *Outcasts from Evolution: Scientific Attitudes of Race Inferiority, 1859-1900*. Champaign: University of Illinois Press.
An account of the persistence of racist views in post-Darwinian anthropology.

Hawkins, Mike (1997) *Social Darwinism in European and American Thought, 1860-1945: Nature as Model and Nature as Threat*. New York: Cambridge University Press.
An interpretive history of Social Darwinism in Euro-American culture.

Himmelfarb, Gertrude (1959) *Darwin and the Darwinian Revolution*. London: Chatto and Windus.
An analysis of Darwinism as an expression of its social time and place.

Hofstadter, Richard (1992) [1944] *Social Darwinism in American Thought*. Boston: Beacon Press.
An analysis of Social Darwinism in America in the decades after *Origin of Species*.

Lyell, Charles (1970) [1830] *Principles of Geology*. Forestburgh, New York: Lubrecht and Cramer.
Lyell's landmark treatise on uniformitarian geology.

Mayr, Ernst (1990) *The Growth of Biological Thought: Diversity, Evolution and Inheritance*. Cambridge, Massachusetts: The Belknap Press of Harvard University.
A masterful history of biology by one of the architects of the twentieth-century synthetic theory of evolution.

Mayr, Ernst (1991) *One Long Argument: Charles Darwin and the Genesis of Modern Evolutionary Thought*. Cambridge, Massachusetts: Harvard University Press.
An exposition of the Darwinian origins of evolutionism.

McCown, Theodore D., and Kenneth A. R. Kennedy (Eds.) (1972) *Climbing Man's Family Tree: A Collection of Major Writings on Human Phylogeny, 1699-1971*. Englewood Cliffs, New Jersey: Prentice-Hall.
A collection of interpretations of human evolution spanning three centuries.

Millhauser, Milton (1959) *Just Before Darwin: Robert Chambers and Vestiges*. Middletown, Connecticut: Wesleyan University Press.
A scientific biography of one of the most notable pre-Darwinian evolutionists.

Olby, Robert C. (1995) *The Origins of Mendelism*. Chicago: University of Chicago Press.
A history of early modern genetics and hereditarian outlooks in science.

Oldroyd, David R. (1996) *Thinking About the Earth: A History of Ideas in Geology*. Cambridge, Massachusetts: Harvard University Press.
An intellectual history of geology by a respected historian of science.

Ruse, Michael (1997) *Monad to Man: The Concept of Progress in Evolutionary Biology*. Cambridge, Massachusetts: Harvard University Press.
A history of biology linked to the idea of progress.

Schiller, Francis (1992) *Paul Broca: Founder of French Anthropology, Explorer of the Brain*. New York: Oxford University Press.
An intellectual biography of the leading French physical anthropologist of the nineteenth century.

Spencer, Frank (Comp.) (1986) *Ecce Homo: An Annotated Bibliographic History of Physical Anthropology*. Westport, Connecticut: Greenwood.
A major sourcebook compiled by a leading historian of physical anthropology.

Spencer, Frank (Ed.) (1997) *History of Physical Anthropology: An Encyclopedia*. New York: Garland.
A comprehensive two-volume encyclopedic history of physical anthropology.

Stanton, William Ragan (1960) *The Leopard's Spots: Scientific Attitudes Toward Race in America, 1815-1859*. Chicago: University of Chicago Press.
A history of American anthropology in the first half of the nineteenth century, highlighting the "American School."

Stocking, George W., Jr. (1982) *Race, Culture and Evolution: Essays in the History of Anthropology*. Chicago: University of Chicago Press.
An analysis of important themes in nineteenth- and twentieth-century anthropology.

Stocking, George W., Jr. (Ed.) (1990) *Bones, Bodies, and Behavior: Essays on Biological Anthropology*. Madison: University of Wisconsin Press.
A collection of articles on a wide range of topics in the history of physical anthropology.

Young, Robert M. (1985) *Darwin's Metaphor: Nature's Place in Victorian Culture.* New York: Cambridge University Press.

An examination of the conceptualization of "nature" in nineteenth-century science and culture.

Franz Boas

Barrett, Stanley R. (1996) *Anthropology: A Student's Guide to Theory and Method.* Toronto: University of Toronto Press.

An exposition of major twentieth-century theories and methods, accompanied by ethnographic examples derived from the author's own fieldwork.

Boas, Franz (1989) *A Franz Boas Reader: The Shaping of American Anthropology, 1883-1911.* George W. Stocking, Jr., ed. Chicago: University of Chicago Press.

A book that places major works of Boas in historical perspective.

Deacon, Desley (1997) *Elsie Clews Parsons: Inventing Modern Life.* Chicago: University of Chicago Press.

A biography of a pioneering American social theorist who was a patron of Boasian anthropologists.

Gacs, Ute *et al.* (Eds.) (1988) *Women Anthropologists: A Biographical Dictionary.* New York: Greenwood Press.

Sketches of numerous women in all fields of modern anthropology, including backgrounds and professional accomplishments.

Hare, Peter H. (1985) *A Woman's Quest for Science: A Portrait of Anthropologist Elsie Clews Parsons.* Amherst, New York: Prometheus Books.

Another biography of Parsons.

Helm, June (Ed.) (1988) *Pioneers of American Anthropology: The Uses of Biography.* New York: AMS Press.

Biographical accounts of early American anthropologists.

Hemenway, Robert E. (1980) *Zora Neale Hurston: A Literary Biography*. Urbana: University of Illinois Press.
A biography of an African-American student of Boas and acclaimed author and folklorist.

Herskovits, Melville J. (1953) *Franz Boas*. New York: Scribner.
A biography of Boas by an accomplished Boasian anthropologist.

Hyatt, Marshall (1990) *Franz Boas, Social Activist: The Dynamics of Ethnicity*. New York: Greenwood Press.
A biographical account of Boas' involvement with social issues pertaining to the anthropological understanding of ethnicity.

Linton, Adelin, and Charles Wagley (1971) *Ralph Linton*. New York: Columbia University Press.
A biography of an accomplished Boasian-era anthropologist.

Murra, John V. (Ed.) (1976) *American Anthropology: The Early Years*. St. Paul, Minnesota: West.
A collection of articles about pioneering American anthropologists.

Silverman, Sydel (Ed.) (1981) *Totems and Teachers: Perspectives on the History of Anthropology*. New York: Columbia University Press.
Accounts of the history of anthropology shaped by the relationship between prominent students and teachers.

Stocking, George W., Jr. (Ed.) (1985) *Observers Observed: Essays on Ethnographic Fieldwork*. Madison: University of Wisconsin Press.
A collection of articles about the history of ethnographic fieldwork.

Stocking, George W., Jr. (Ed.) (1996) *Volksgeist as Method and Ethic: Essays on Boasian Ethnography and the German Anthropological Tradition*. Madison: University of Wisconsin Press.
A collection of articles about Boas' German background and its effect on his ethnography.

Thoresen, Timothy H. (Ed.) (1975) *Toward a Science of Man: Essays in the History of Anthropology*. Hawthorne, New York: Mouton de Gruyter.
A collection of articles highlighting the contributions of Boas and his students.

Williams, Vernon J., Jr. (1996) *Rethinking Race: Franz Boas and His Contemporaries*. Lexington: University Press of Kentucky.
Assessments of the efforts of Boas and his contemporaries to overcome an anthropological legacy of racism.

Robert Lowie and Alfred Louis Kroeber

Driver, Harold Edson (1962) *The Contribution of A. L. Kroeber to Culture Area Theory and Practice*. Baltimore: Waverly Press.
An American Indianist anthropologist recounts Kroeber's contributions to American Indian anthropology.

Kroeber, A.L. (1944) *Configurations of Cultural Growth*. Berkeley: University of California Press.
Kroeber's *magnum opus*.

Kroeber, Theodora (1970) *Alfred Kroeber: A Personal Configuration*. Berkeley: University of California Press.
A loving biography of Kroeber by his wife.

Lowie, Robert H. (1937) *History of Ethnological Theory*. New York: Rinehart and Company.
Lowie contrasts Boasian ethnology with the ethnology of his nineteenth-century predecessors.

Lowie, Robert H. [1959] *Robert H. Lowie, Ethnologist: A Personal Record*. Ann Arbor, Michigan: Books on Demand.
Lowie's autobiography.

Lowie, Robert (1960) [1920] *Primitive Society*. London: Routledge and Kegan Paul.

Lowie's summation of anthropology contrasted with the summations of nine-teenth-century evolutionists.

Murphy, Robert Francis (1972) *Robert H. Lowie*. New York: Columbia University Press.

A biography of Lowie by an accomplished American anthropologist.

Steward, Julian Haines (1973) *Alfred Kroeber*. New York: Columbia University Press.

A biography of Kroeber by a distinguished cultural ecologist and evolutionist.

Winters, Christopher (Ed.) (1991) *International Dictionary of Anthropologists*. New York: Garland.

A source book of information on American and other national anthropologists of the modern era, including backgrounds and professional accomplishments.

Margaret Mead and Ruth Benedict

Bateson, Mary C. (1994) [1984] *With a Daughter's Eye: A Memoir of Gregory Bateson and Margaret Mead*. New York: Harper Collins.

A biography of Mead and her third husband by their daughter.

Benedict, Ruth (1977) *An Anthropologist at Work: The Writings of Ruth Benedict*. Margaret Mead, ed. Westport, Connecticut: Greenwood.

A collection of key writings by Benedict edited by her long-time friend and colleague.

Benedict, Ruth (1989) [1934] *Patterns of Culture*. Boston: Houghton Mifflin.

Benedict's classic analysis of three cultures, for decades an anthropology best-seller.

Caffrey, Margaret M. (1989) *Ruth Benedict: Stranger in this Land*. Austin: University of Texas Press.
A biography of Benedict that explores her sense of personal and cultural alienation.

Cassidy, Robert (1982) *Margaret Mead: A Voice for the Century*. New York: Universe Books.
A biography of Mead highlighting her ability to communicate with the public.

Cote, James E. (1994) *Adolescent Storm and Stress: An Evaluation of the Mead-Freeman Controversy*. Mahwah, New Jersey: Laurence Erlbaum Associates.
A contribution to the anthropological debate about Mead's ethnographic work in Samoa.

Cressman, Luther S. (1988) *A Golden Journey: Memoirs of an Archaeologist*. Ann Arbor, Michigan: Books on Demand.
A book in which Cressman shows why he should be remembered as more than Margaret Mead's first husband.

Foerstel, Lenora, and Angela Gilliam (Eds.) (1991) *Confronting the Margaret Mead Legacy: Scholarship, Empire and South Pacific*. Philadelphia: Temple University Press.
Examinations of Mead's legacy to anthropology.

Freeman, Derek [1982] *Margaret Mead and Samoa: The Making and Unmaking of an Anthropological Myth*. Ann Arbor, Michigan: Books on Demand.
The book that began a protracted anthropological debate about Mead's ethnographic work in Samoa.

Grosskurth, Phillis (1988) *Margaret Mead: A Life*. London: Penguin Books.
A biography of Mead written to appeal to the public.

Holmes, Lowell D. (1986) *Quest for the Real Samoa: The Mead-Freeman Controversy and Beyond.* Westport, Connecticut: Greenwood.
A contribution to the anthropological debate about Mead's ethnographic work in Samoa.

Howard, Jane (1984) *Margaret Mead: A Life.* New York: Simon and Schuster.
A biography of Mead written to appeal to the public.

Lipset, David (1980) *Gregory Bateson: The Legacy of a Scientist.* Englewood Cliffs, New Jersey: Prentice-Hall.
A biography of Mead's third husband and the scientist responsible for the "double-bind" theory of schizophrenia.

Mead, Margaret (1974) *Ruth Benedict.* New York: Columbia University Press.
A biography of Benedict by her long-time friend and colleague.

Mead, Margaret (1990) [1972] *Blackberry Winter.* Magnolia, Massachusetts: Peter Smith.
The first volume of Mead's projected multi-volume autobiography.

Mead, Margaret (1990) [1928] *Coming of Age in Samoa.* Magnolia, Massachusetts: Peter Smith.
The book that launched Mead's career.

Modell, Judith Schachter (1983) *Ruth Benedict: Patterns of a Life.* Philadelphia: University of Pennsylvania Press.
A biography of Benedict that explores her personal interest in cultural patterns.

Orans, Martin (1996) *Not Even Wrong: Margaret Mead, Derek Freeman, and the Samoans.* L.L. Langness and Robert B. Edgerton, eds. Novato, California: Chandler and Sharp.
A contribution to the anthropological debate about Mead's ethnographic work in Samoa.

Parezo, Nancy J. (Ed.) (1993) *Hidden Scholars: Women Anthropologists and the Native American Southwest.* Albuquerque: University of New Mexico Press.
A collection of articles highlighting contributions of women anthropologists working in the American Southwest.

Rice, Edward (1979) *Margaret Mead: A Portrait.* New York: Harper and Row.
A biography of Mead written to appeal to the public.

The Influence of Sigmund Freud

Freud, Sigmund (1960) [1913] *Totem and Taboo.* Abraham A. Brill, trans. New York: Random House.
Freud's anthropological speculations on the origin of the conflict between culture and the human psyche.

Freud, Sigmund (1973) [1928] *The Future of an Illusion.* James Strachey, rev. and ed. London: Hogarth Press and the Institute of Psycho-Analysis.
Freud's further thoughts on the conflict between culture and the human psyche.

Gilman, Sander L. (1993) *Freud, Race, and Gender.* Princeton, New Jersey: Princeton University Press.
An examination of anthropological themes in Freudianism.

Ritvo, Lucile B. (1990) *Darwin's Influence on Freud: A Tale of Two Sciences.* New Haven, Connecticut: Yale University Press.
Histories of nineteenth- and twentieth-century Darwinian biology and Freudian psychology.

Wallace, Edwin R., IV (1983) *Freud and Anthropology: A History and Reappraisal.* Madison, Connecticut: International Universities Press.
A critical examination of the relationship between Freudian psychology and anthropology.

Development of Psychological Anthropology

Chasdi, Eleanor H. (Ed.) (1994) *Culture and Human Development: The Selected Papers of John Whiting*. New York: Cambridge University Press.
Key papers of an anthropologist who advanced psychological anthropology in the post-Second World War period.

Du Bois, Cora (1944) *The People of Alor: A Social-Psychological Study of an East-Indian Island*. Minneapolis: University of Minnesota Press.
A prime example of psychodynamic ethnology.

Honigmann, John J. [1975] *The Development of Anthropological Ideas*. Ann Arbor, Michigan: Books on Demand.
A history of anthropology with an emphasis on psychological anthropology.

Kardiner, Abram, and Edward Preble (1961) *They Studied Man*. Cleveland, Ohio: World Publishing Company.
Biographical sketches of prominent early anthropologists, accompanied by an essay on the contributions of Sigmund Freud.

Kroeber, A. L., and Clyde Kluckhohn (1952) *Culture: A Critical Review of Concepts and Definitions*. Cambridge, Massachusetts: Peabody Museum of American Archaeology and Ethnology.
A compendium of conceptualizations of culture by two anthropologists who conceptualized culture as shared values.

Manson, William C. (1988) *The Psychodynamics of Culture: Abram Kardiner and Neo-Freudian Anthropology*. Westport, Connecticut: Greenwood.
An examination of the life and work of the chief architect of psychodynamic anthropology.

Rigdon, Susan M. (1988) *The Culture Facade: Art, Science and Politics in the Work of Oscar Lewis*. Champaign: University of Illinois Press.
A biography of a twentieth-century anthropologist who studied the culture of poverty.

Simpson, George Eaton (1973) *Melville J. Herskovits*. New York: Columbia University Press.
A biography of a Boasian-era anthropologist who studied African-American culture.

Spindler, George Dearborn (Ed.) (1978) *The Making of Psychological Anthropology*. Berkeley: University of California Press.
Assessments of the foundations of psychological anthropology.

Spiro, Melford E. (1992) *Oedipus in the Trobriands*. New Brunswick, New Jersey: Transaction.
An account of Bronislaw Malinowski's investigation of Freudian psychology in the Trobriand Islands.

Stocking, George W., Jr. (Ed.) (1986) *Malinowski, Rivers, Benedict and Others: Essays on Culture and Personality*. Madison: University of Wisconsin Press.
A collection of articles exploring themes in psychological anthropology.

Taylor, Walter W., John Fischer, and Evon Z. Vogt (Eds.) (1973) *Culture and Life: Essays in Memory of Clyde Kluckhohn*. Carbondale: Southern Illinois University Press.
Commemorations of the work of an American anthropologist interested in cross-cultural values.

Whiting, John W., and Irvin I. Child (1984) [1953] *Child-Training and Personality: A Cross-Cultural Study*. Westport, Connecticut: Greenwood.
A landmark cross-cultural study of culture and personality.

The Influence of Émile Durkheim

Besnard, Philippe (Ed.) (1983) *The Sociological Domain, the Durkheimians and the Founding of French Sociology*. Cambridge: Cambridge University Press.
Examinations of Durkheim's role in shaping French sociology.

Durkheim, Émile (1966) [1897] *Suicide*. New York: The Free Press.
Durkheim analyzes suicide from his sociological perspective.

Durkheim, Émile (1982) [1895] *The Rules of Sociological Method*. New York: The Free Press.
Durkheim explains the importance of social facts.

Durkheim, Émile (1984) [1893] *The Division of Labor in Society*. W.D. Hall, trans. New York: The Free Press.
Durkheim explains the distinction between mechanical and organic social solidarity.

Durkheim, Émile (1995) [1912] *The Elementary Forms of the Religious Life*. Karen E. Fields, trans. New York: The Free Press.
Durkheim analyzes the collective consciousness.

Hilbert, Richard A. (1992) *The Classical Roots of Ethnomethodology: Durkheim, Weber and Garfinkel*. Chapel Hill: University of North Carolina Press.
An examination of the contributions of Durkheim and other theorists to ethnomethodology.

Jones, Robert A. (1986) *The Sociological Theories of Émile Durkheim*. Thousand Oaks, California: Sage Publications.
An assessment of Durkheim's sociology.

Lukes, Steven (1985) *Émile Durkheim: His Life and Work: A Historical and Critical Study*. Stanford, California: Stanford University Press.
An interpretation of Durkheim's intellectual life and times.

Parkin, Frank (1992) *Durkheim*. Oxford: Oxford University Press.
A biographical account of Durkheim.

Turner, Stephen P. (1993) *Émile Durkheim: Sociologist and Moralist*. New York: Routledge.
An evaluation of Durkheim as a moralist.

French Structural Anthropology

Boon, James A. (1972) *From Symbolism to Structuralism: Lévi-Strauss in a Literary Tradition.* New York: Harper and Row.
An analysis of Lévi-Strauss as a literary figure.

Champagne, Roland (1987) *Claude Lévi-Strauss.* Old Tappan, New Jersey: Scribner's Reference.
A biographical study of Lévi-Strauss.

Henaff, Marcel (1991) *Claude Lévi-Strauss.* Paris: Belfond.
The life and work of Lévi-Strauss.

Jenkins, Alan (1979) *The Social Theory of Claude Lévi-Strauss.* London: Macmillan.
An account of key theoretical elements of French structural anthropology.

Leach, Edmund R. (1989) [1970] *Claude Lévi-Strauss.* Chicago: University of Chicago Press.
An assessment of the work of Lévi-Strauss by a distinguished British social anthropologist.

Lévi-Strauss, Claude (1969) *Elementary Structures of Kinship.* James Harlebell *et al.*, eds. Boston: Beacon Press.
Lévi-Strauss' seminal structural analysis of kinship.

Lévi-Strauss, Claude (1974) [1963] *Structural Anthropology.* New York: Basic Books.
Lévi-Strauss' exposition of structuralism.

Mauss, Marcel (1990) [1924] *Gift: The Form and Reason for Exchange in Archaic Societies.* New York: W.W. Norton.
The book from which Lévi-Strauss derived part of his theory of reciprocity.

Rossi, Ino (Ed.) (1974) *The Unconscious in Culture: The Structuralism of Claude Lévi-Strauss in Perspective*. New York: Dutton.
Expositions of Lévi-Strauss' structuralism.

Sahlins, Marshall (1987) *Islands of History*. Chicago: University of Chicago Press.
Sahlins promulgates his view that "structure" is the historically objectified relations of cultural order.

Stocking, George W., Jr. (Ed.) (1996) *Romantic Motives: Essays on Anthropological Sensibility*. Madison: University of Wisconsin Press.
Accounts of anthropological styles, some French.

British Social Anthropology

Douglas, Mary (1980) *Edward Evans-Pritchard*. New York: Viking Press.
A biography of a distinguished British social anthropologist known for his ethnographic work among the Nuer of Africa.

Ellen, Roy *et al.* (Eds.) (1989) *Malinowski: Between Two Worlds: The Polish Roots of an Anthropological Tradition*. New York: Cambridge University Press.
Investigations of the Polish background of Bronislaw Malinowski.

Goody, Jack (1995) *The Expansive Moment: The Rise of Social Anthropology in Britain and Africa, 1918-1970*. New York: Cambridge University Press.
A history of British social anthropology highlighting its African connection.

Henson, Hilary (1974) *British Social Anthropologists and Language: A History of Separate Development*. Oxford: Clarendon Press.
An examination of the relationship between social and linguistic anthropology in Britain.

Hiatt, L. R. (1996) *Arguments about Aborigines: Australia and the Evolution of Social Anthropology*. New York: Cambridge University Press.
An examination of the development of social anthropology in Australia.

Kuklik, Henrika (1992) *The Savage Within: The Social History of British Anthropology, 1885-1945*. New York: Cambridge University Press.
A contextual history of British social anthropology in its heyday.

Kuper, Adam (1983) *Anthropology and Anthropologists: The Modern British School*. Rev. ed. New York: Routledge.
An informative history of British social anthropology.

Langham, Ian G. (1981) *The Building of British Social Anthropology*. Norwell, Massachusetts: Kluwer Academic Publishers.
A history of the foundations of British social anthropology.

Malinowski, Bronislaw (1984) [1922] *Argonauts of the Western Pacific*. Prospect Heights, Illinois: Waveland Press, Inc.
Malinowski's critically acclaimed ethnography of Trobriand Islanders.

Malinowski, Bronislaw (1989) [1967] *A Diary in the Strict Sense of the Term*. Stanford, California: Stanford University Press.
Malinowski's controversial diary of his fieldwork experiences.

Marcus, Julie (Ed.) (1993) *First in Their Field: Women and Australian Anthropology*. Concord, Massachusetts: Paul and Company Publishers Consortium.
Assessments of the importance of female Australian anthropologists.

Radcliffe-Brown, A. R. (1964) [1922] *The Andaman Islanders*. New York: Free Press of Glencoe.
Radcliffe-Brown's highly regarded ethnography.

Radcliffe-Brown, A. R. (1965) [1952] *Structure and Function in Primitive Society*. New York: The Free Press.
Radcliffe-Brown's exposition of structuralism and functionalism.

Slobodin, Richard (1978) *W.H.R. Rivers*. New York: Columbia University Press.
A biography of the British anthropologist who pioneered the genealogical method of fieldwork.

Stocking, George W., Jr. (1992) *The Ethnographer's Magic and Other Essays in the History of Anthropology*. Madison: University of Wisconsin Press.
A collection of essays about fieldwork and related anthropological topics.

Stocking, George W., Jr. (1995) *After Tylor: British Social Anthropology, 1888-1951*. Madison: University of Wisconsin Press.
An authoritative history of British social anthropology in the first half of the twentieth century.

Stocking, George W., Jr. (Ed.) (1984) *Functionalism Historicized: Essays on British Social Anthropology*. Madison: University of Wisconsin Press.
A collection of essays on British social anthropology highlighting functionalism.

Strenski, Ivan (1992) *Malinowski and the Work of Myth*. Princeton, New Jersey: Princeton University Press.
An assessment of Malinowski's contributions to the anthropological study of myth.

Urry, James (Ed.) (1993) *Before Social Anthropology: Essays on the History of British Anthropology*. Newark, New Jersey: Gordon and Breach.
A collection of essays on early modern British anthropology.

Vermeulen, Han, and Artura A. Roldan (Eds.) (1995) *Fieldwork and Footnotes: Studies in the History of European Anthropology*. New York: Routledge.
A collection of articles about the history of anthropological traditions in Europe.

The Legacy of Max Weber

Comaroff, Jean, and John L. Comaroff (1991) *Of Revelation and Revolution, Vol. 1: Christianity, Colonialism, and Consciousness in South Africa.* Chicago: University of Chicago Press.
In this recently influential work of "historical ethnography," the Comaroffs present an explicitly Weberian study of the colonial inscription of European culture on the inhabitants and landscape of South Africa in the eighteenth and nineteenth centuries.

Wallace, Anthony F. (1966) *Religion: An Anthropological View.* New York: Random House.
In this book, Wallace develops his theoretical perspective on religion, and in particular its capacity to effect personal psychological "mazeway transformation" and social "revitalization" in response to cultural stress or dissonance.

Wallace, Anthony F. (1972) *The Death and Rebirth of the Seneca.* New York: Random House.
Now a classic in its own right, Wallace's very readable study of colonization and social change among the Seneca nation of eastern North America combines Durkheimian and Weberian perspectives to show how one integrated cultural system was first disrupted, then reformulated in response to the colonial encounter of the post-Renaissance era.

Weber, Max (1993) [1922] *The Sociology of Religion.* Boston: Beacon Press.
In this classic work of sociology, Weber outlines his formulation of religion and religious phenomena, paying special attention to the ways in which these effect social change in a variety of cultural and historical settings.

Weber, Max (1996) [1920] *The Protestant Ethic and the Spirit of Capitalism.* Randall Collins, ed. Los Angeles: Roxbury.
Written at an earlier date than *The Sociology of Religion*, much of Weber's thesis here is recapitulated in the later work. This book looks at the dialectical relationship between Calvinist Protestantism as an ideology and the expansion of capitalism in the Renaissance era and beyond.

Worsley, Peter (1968) *The Trumpet Shall Sound*. New York: Schocken Books.
In this account of "cargo cults" in the South Pacific, Worsley writes from a distinctly Weberian perspective. He argues that the great variety of ecstatic religious movements found in the region are the product of a colonial encounter that disrupted local economies, religious beliefs and ritual, and political arrangements.

Cognitive Anthropology

Aarsleff, Hans (1982) *From Locke to Saussure: Essays on the Study of Language and Intellectual History*. Minneapolis: University of Minnesota Press.
A history of linguistics beginning in the late seventeenth century.

Carroll, J. B. (Ed.) (1956) *Language, Thought and Reality: Selected Writings of Benjamin Lee Whorf*. New York: John Wiley and Sons.
A collection of key writings by the co-formulator of the Sapir-Whorf hypothesis.

D'Andrade, Roy (1995) *The Development of Cognitive Anthropology*. New York: Cambridge University Press.
An exposition of cognitive anthropology in historical perspective.

Darnell, Regna (1990) *Edward Sapir: Linguist, Anthropologist, Humanist*. Berkeley: University of California Press.
A biography of the distinguished Boasian anthropologist and co-formulator of the Sapir-Whorf hypothesis.

Hall, Robert A. (1987) *Leonard Bloomfield: Essays on His Life and Work*. Philadelphia: John Benjamins.
Evaluations of the work of a twentieth-century linguist who pioneered phonemic analysis.

Hymes, Dell (1983) *Essays in the History of Linguistic Anthropology*. Philadelphia: John Benjamins North America.
A distinguished anthropological linguist writes about the history of his subject.

Hymes, Dell (Ed.) (1974) *Studies in the History of Linguistics: Traditions and Paradigms*. Ann Arbor, Michigan: Books on Demand.
A major collection of articles about themes in the history of linguistics.

Pike, Eunice (1981) *Ken Pike: Scholar and Christian*. Dallas: Summer Institute of Linguistics, Academic Publications.
A biographical account of the linguist who helped formulate the distinction between emics and etics.

Sapir, Edward (1958) *Culture, Language and Personality: Selected Essays*. David Mandelbaum, ed. Berkeley: University of California Press.
A collection of essays on the relationship between language, culture, and personality by the leading anthropological linguist of the Boasian era.

Sebeok, Thomas Albert (Ed.) (1966) *Portraits of Linguistics: A Biographical Source Book for the History of Western Linguistics, 1746-1963*. Bloomington: Indiana University Press.
A valuable source of information about linguists of the last two centuries.

Tyler, Stephen (1969) *Cognitive Anthropology*. New York: Holt, Rinehart, and Winston.
A book about cognitive anthropology written in its heyday.

Cultural Neo-Evolutionism

Binford, Lewis R. (1983) *In Pursuit of the Past*. London: Thames and Hudson.
An exposition of the New Archaeology by the leading New Archaeologist.

Bohannan, Paul and Mark Glazer (Eds.) (1989) *High Points in Anthropology*. 2nd ed. New York: McGraw-Hill.
A collection of writings by influential anthropologists of the nineteenth and twentieth centuries.

Fried, Morton H. (1967) *The Evolution of Political Society: An Evolutionary View*. New York: The McGraw-Hill Companies.
Variation in political organization explained in evolutionary terms.

Green, Sally (1981) *Prehistorian: A Biography of V. Gordon Childe*. Bradford-on-Avon: The Moonraker Press.
A biography of the maverick "Marxist" archaeologist who described Neolithic and urban "revolutions."

Harris, David R. (Ed.) (1994) *The Archaeology of V. Gordon Childe*. Concord, Massachusetts: Paul and Company Publishers Consortium.
A collection of articles evaluating Childe's contributions to archaeology.

Manners, Robert Alan (Ed.) (1964) *Process and Pattern in Culture, Essays in Honor of Julian Steward*. Chicago: Aldine Publishing Company.
Examinations of Julian Steward's role in the development of cultural ecology and evolution.

McNairn, Barbara (1980) *The Method and Theory of V. Gordon Childe*. Edinburgh: Edinburgh University Press.
An intellectual biography of Childe.

Patterson, Thomas C. (1994) *Toward a Social History of Archaeology in the United States*. Jeffrey Quilter, ed. Orlando, Florida: Harcourt Brace College Publishers.
A history of American archaeology in social contexts.

Pinsky, Valerie, and Alison Wylie (Eds.) (1995) *Critical Traditions in Contemporary Archaeology: Essays in the Philosophy, History and Socio-Politics of Archaeology*. Albuquerque: University of New Mexico Press.
Critical archaeological perspectives.

Reyman, Jonathan E. (Ed.) (1992) *Rediscovering Our Past: Essays on the History of American Archaeology*. Avebury, England: Aldershot.
A collection of articles representing new views on the history of American archaeology.

Sahlins, Marshall D., and Elman R. Service (Eds.) (1960) *Evolution and Culture*. Ann Arbor: University of Michigan Press.
Sahlins and Service reconcile the evolutionary theories of Julian Steward and Leslie White.

Service, Elman R. (1962) *Primitive Social Organization: An Evolutionary Perspective*. New York: Random House.
Variation in social organization explained in evolutionary terms.

Service, Elman R. (1985) *A Century of Controversy*. Orlando, Florida: Academic Press.
A history of ethnology written by a prominent cultural neo-evolutionist.

Steward, Julian (1972) [1955] *Theory of Culture Change: The Methodology of Multilinear Evolution*. Champaign: University of Illinois Press.
Steward's explanation of cultural evolution contrasted with the explanations of Leslie White and others.

Trigger, Bruce G. (1980) *Gordon Childe: Revolutions in Archaeology*. New York: Columbia University Press.
A biography of Childe by a respected historian of archaeology.

White, Leslie A. (1949) *The Science of Culture*. New York: Grove Press.
A collection of seminal essays on culturology.

White, Leslie A. (1959) *The Evolution of Culture: The Development of Civilization to the Fall of Rome*. New York: McGraw-Hill.
White's explanation of cultural evolution in terms of thermodynamics and the principles of culturology.

Cultural Materialism

Harris, Marvin (1979) *Cultural Materialism: The Struggle for a Science of Culture*. New York: Random House, Inc.
Harris' cultural materialist manifesto.

Harris, Marvin (1990) [1974] *Cows, Pigs, Wars and Witches: The Riddles of Culture*. New York: Random House.
One of several popular books written by Harris to demonstrate the explanatory power of cultural materialism.

McGee, Jon R., and Richard L. Warms (1996) *Anthropological Theory: An Introductory History*. Mountain View, California: Mayfield.
A collection of annotated writings by prominent anthropologists of the nineteenth and twentieth centuries, including cultural materialists.

Biologized Anthropology

Ardrey, Robert (1961) *African Genesis: A Personal Investigation into the Animal Origins and Nature of Man*. New York: Atheneum.
Ardrey's "popular" views on human evolution and the innateness of human aggression.

Cravens, Hamilton (1988) *The Triumph of Evolution: The Heredity-Environment Controversy, 1900-1941*. Baltimore: Johns Hopkins University Press.
Historical background for exploring "nature versus nurture" in anthropology.

Dawkins, Richard (1989) [1976] *The Selfish Gene*. 2nd ed. New York: Oxford University Press.
Dawkins' "ultra-Darwinist" exposition of evolution, and contribution to sociobiology.

Dunn, Leslie C. (1991) *A Short History of Genetics: The Development of Some of the Main Lines of Thought, 1864-1939*. Ames: Iowa State University Press.
A history of genetics and genetics issues.

Kevles, Daniel J. (1995) [1985] *In the Name of Eugenics: Genetics and the Uses of Human Heredity*. Cambridge, Massachusetts: Harvard University Press.
A history of genetics, eugenics, and related scientific and social issues.

Kuhl, Stefan (1994) *The Nazi Connection: Eugenics, American Racism and German National Socialism*. New York: Oxford University Press.
An examination of the scientific and social underpinnings of German National Socialism.

Larson, Edward J. (1996) *Sex, Race, and Science: Eugenics in the Deep South*. Baltimore: Johns Hopkins University Press.
An examination of eugenics in the American South.

Leakey, L.S.B. (1966) *White African: An Early Autobiography*. Cambridge, Massachusetts: Schenkman.
Louis Leakey's early life in Africa.

Leakey, Mary (1984) *Disclosing the Past: An Autobiography*. New York: Doubleday.
Mary Leakey's autobiography of her life with and without Louis.

Leakey, Richard E. (1984) *One Life: An Autobiography*. Salem, New Hampshire: Salem House.
Richard Leakey's autobiography, written while he was critically ill.

Maasen, Sabine (1995) *Biology as Society, Society as Biology: Metaphors*. Everett Mendelsohn, *et al.*, eds. Norwell, Massachusetts: Kluwer Academic Publishers.
An examination of the interplay among biological and sociological conceptualizations.

McLaren, Angus (1990) *Our Own Master Race: Eugenics in Canada, 1885-1945.* Toronto: McClelland and Stewart.
A history of Canadian eugenics in the late nineteenth and early twentieth centuries.

Morrell, Virginia (1995) *Ancestral Passions: The Leakey Family and the Quest for Humankind's Beginnings.* New York: Simon and Schuster.
Biographies of Louis, Mary, and Richard Leakey.

Morris, Desmond (1980) *The Naked Ape.* New York: Dell Publishing Company.
The book that spawned the phrase "naked apery."

Neel, James V. (1994) *Physician to the Gene Pool: Genetic Lessons and Other Stories.* New York: John Wiley and Sons.
The autobiography of a leading human geneticist.

Nisbet, Alec (1977) *Konrad Lorenz.* New York: Harcourt Brace Jovanovich.
A biography of the pioneering European ethologist.

Poliakov, Leon (1974) *The Aryan Myth: A History of Racist and Nationalist Ideas in Europe.* Edmund Howard, trans. London: Chatto and Windus.
A critical history of Aryanism.

Provine, William B. (1987) *The Origins of Theoretical Population Genetics.* Chicago: University of Chicago Press.
A book for the mathematically inclined.

Ruse, Michael (1984) *Sociobiology: Sense or Nonsense?.* Rev. ed. Norwell, Massachusetts: Kluwer Academic Publishers.
A critique of sociobiology by a well-known philosopher of science.

Sahlins, Marshall (1976) *The Use and Abuse of Biology: An Anthropological Critique of Sociobiology.* Ann Arbor: University of Michigan Press.
An early negative critique of the sociobiological perspective in anthropology.

Shipman, Pat (1994) *Evolution of Racism: The Human Difference and the Use and Abuse of Science*. New York: Simon and Schuster.
A scientific critique of racism by a respected physical anthropologist.

Spencer, Frank (1990) *Piltdown: A Scientific Forgery*. New York: Oxford University Press.
The story of a famous whodunit.

Spencer, Frank (Ed.) (1982) *A History of American Physical Anthropology, 1930-1980*. New York: Academic Press.
Histories of American physical anthropology in the mid-twentieth century.

Thorpe, W.H. (1979) *The Origins and Rise of Ethology*. Westport, Connecticut: Greenwood.
A history of ethological approaches to the study of animal, including human, behaviour.

Wilson, Edward O. (1975) *Sociobiology: The New Synthesis*. Cambridge, Massachusetts: Belknap Press of Harvard University.
The book that introduced sociobiology to science and society.

Wilson, Edward O. (1994) *Naturalist*. Washington, D.C.: Island Press.
An autobiography of the founder of sociobiology.

Wilson, Edward O. (1994) *On Human Nature*. Cambridge, Massachusetts: Harvard University Press.
A discussion of the relevance of sociobiology to *Homo sapiens*.

Wolpoff, Milford and Rachel Caspari (1997) *Race and Human Evolution: A Fatal Attraction*. New York: Simon and Schuster.
An examination of historical relationships among theories of race and human evolution.

Symbolic and Interpretive Anthropology

Geertz, Clifford (1977) [1973] *Interpretation of Cultures*. New York: Basic Books.
The classic treatise of American "interpretive anthropology," which contains (among others) Geertz' influential essays about "thick description," religion as a "cultural system," and the analysis of a Balinese cockfight.

Geertz, Clifford (1996) *After the Fact: Two Countries, Four Decades, One Anthropologist*. Cambridge, Massachusetts: Harvard University Press.
Geertz' autobiography.

Hodder, Ian (1986) *Reading the Past: Current Approaches to Interpretation in Archaeology*. Cambridge: Cambridge University Press.
An exposition of post-processual archaeology by a leading post-processualist.

Schneider, David M. (1980) *American Kinship: A Cultural Account*. Chicago: University of Chicago Press.
In this well-known "interpretive" account of kinship, Schneider advocates a more "structuralist" approach to understanding symbols and looks to the coherence and logic behind the symbolic "system" first described by Geertz.

Turner, Victor (1967) *The Forest of Symbols: Aspects of Ndembu Ritual*. Ithaca, New York: Cornell University Press.
In this prototypical ethnography of the symbolic "school," Turner employs an instrumental theory of Ndembu symbols to show how they are effective in producing certain ritual transformations, which ultimately result in social cohesion.

Turner, Victor (1969) *The Ritual Process: Structure and Anti-Structure*. Hawthorne, New York: Aldine de Gruyter.
In this work, Turner presents his influential re-working of van Gennep's thesis concerning ritual transformation.

van Gennep, Arnold (1961) [1959] *The Rites of Passage*. Monika B. Vizedon and Gabrielle L. Caffee, trans. Chicago: University of Chicago Press.
Van Gennep's original formulation of the "liminal" transition from one social state to another, as accomplished in and by religious ritual.

Political Economy

Dirks, Nicholas B., Geoff Eley, and Sherry B. Ortner (Eds.) (1993) *Culture/Power/History: A Reader in Contemporary Social Theory*. Princeton, New Jersey: Princeton University Press.
A collection of essays on the recent history of anthropology, including one by Ortner that is very useful for situating the theoretical developments that led to the rise of political economy in the 1970s.

Mintz, Sidney W. (1986) *Sweetness and Power: The Place of Sugar in Modern History*. New York: Penguin Books.
Mintz' work is a fascinating historical study of the powerful effect that sugar and the sugar-trade have had in forming new European cultural meanings, and political and economic relationships.

Redfield, Robert (1971) [1956] *Peasant Society and Culture: An Anthropological Approach to Civilization*. Chicago: University of Chicago Press.
Redfield's proto-political economy looks at the continuum between "folk" and "urban" traditions in Mexico.

Roseberry, William (1989) *Anthropologies and Histories: Essays in Culture, History, and Political Economy*. New Brunswick, New Jersey: Rutgers University Press.
In this well-known collection of essays, Roseberry looks at the relationship between capitalism and the historical formation of social and political power, and at the role power has played in shaping cultural meaning and practice.

Schneider, Peter, and Jane Schneider (1986) *Culture and Political Economy in Western Sicily*. Orlando, Florida: Academic Press.

In this classic European ethnography, the Schneiders explore the way in which rural Italian underdevelopment, and alienation of the south from the north, produced local conditions in which new forms of local economy could flourish — in particular the Sicilian Mafia.

Wallerstein, Immanuel (1974) *The Modern World System: Capitalist Agriculture and the Origins of the World Economy in the Sixteenth Century*. Orlando, Florida: Academic Press.

Wallerstein's influential exposition of the expansive capitalist "world system," cast in terms of a "core" of consumers who control and exploit the labour and resources of a poor "periphery."

Wolf, Eric R. (1982) *Europe and the People Without History*. Berkeley: University of California Press.

In this well-known study, Wolf draws on the ideas of Immanuel Wallerstein and Andre Gunder Frank to argue that local cultures around the world are not self-contained, but develop in a dialectical relationship with the expansive forces of global capitalism.

Postmodernism

Anderson, Benedict (1991) *Imagined Communities: Reflections on the Origin and Spread of Nationalism*. London: Verso.

Anderson's influential work examines the broad historical conditions (notably the development of print-capitalism and the post-medieval voyages of discovery) that allowed nation-states to become "imagined" as new forms of community in Europe and its colonies.

Berger, Peter L., and Thomas Luckmann (1967) *The Social Construction of Reality: A Treatise in the Sociology of Knowledge*. New York: Doubleday.
Berger and Luckmann's sociology views the "real" as being the non-objective product of constructive processes (mainly language-related) in which people participate during daily life.

Bourdieu, Pierre (1977) *Outline of a Theory of Practice*. Richard Nice, trans. New York: Cambridge University Press.
This book is Bourdieu's most well-known formulation of his theory of "practice," in which social unity and diversity are produced by creative, historically-situated agents who actively structure and re-structure their worlds of experience.

Clifford, James (1988) *The Predicament of Culture: Twentieth-Century Ethnography, Literature, and Art*. Cambridge, Massachusetts: Harvard University Press.
In this work, Clifford reflects upon the increasingly difficult task with which anthropologists are burdened. The possibility of an "objective" description of culture, and even its very definition or identification, are undermined by the powerful insight that ethnographies are textual artifice.

Clifford, James, and George E. Marcus (Eds.) (1986) *Writing Culture: The Poetics and Politics of Ethnography*. Berkeley: University of California Press.
This highly-influential collection of essays alerted anthropologists to the problematic character of "objectivist" research. Instead, the contributors share a common perspective in regarding ethnographies as cultural "texts," in which the author's own subjectivities are deeply embedded, and in which a range of rhetorical strategies are employed to imbue the subject cultures with the aura of "objectivity."

Foucault, Michel (1982) *The Archaeology of Knowledge*. New York: Pantheon Books.
In this work, Foucault outlines his argument that "knowledge" and "truth" are inexorably linked to social and political power, and that buried beneath the official discourse of modernity and civilization are to be found echoes of dissenting "voices."

Gramsci, Antonio (1992) *Prison Notebooks, Vol. 1.* New York: Columbia University Press.
Gramsci's perspectives on power, written while he was a prisoner, describe the ways in which power inscribes itself on and insinuates its way into social life.

Gramsci, Antonio (1996) *Prison Notebooks, Vol. 2.* Joseph A. Buttigieg, ed. and trans. New York: Columbia University Press.
Gramsci's perspectives on power, written while he was a prisoner, describe the ways in which power inscribes itself on and insinuates its way into social life.

Hobsbawm, Eric J., and Terence Ranger (Eds.) (1992) *The Invention of Tradition.* New York: Cambridge University Press.
This collection of essays looks at the historical process behind the recent production of "ancient" traditions (such as Hugh Trevor-Roper's study of the Scottish kilt), and the general problem of what social purposes might be served by "inventing" history in this way.

Lutz, Catherine (1988) *Unnatural Emotions: Every Day Sentiments on a Micronesian Atoll and Their Challenge to Western Theory.* Chicago: University of Chicago Press.
In Lutz' thought-provoking "postmodern" ethnography of the "emotional" world of a small island in Micronesia, she illuminates the cultural nature of emotions, and so highlights inadequacies in how Western "scientific" theorists have divided the world into the categories of "self" and "other," "rational" and "irrational," and others.

acknowledgements

Chapter I

Adam and Eve. Albrecht Dürer (1471-1528), Nuremburg, Germany, engraving. Centennial gift of Landon T. Clay. Courtesy, Museum of Fine Arts, Boston.

The New World. Justin Winsor, ed., "The Progress of Opinion Respecting the Origin and Antiquity of Man in America," in *Narrative and Critical History of America*, vol I, (369-412) Boston, 1889.

The Old World Meets the New. Attack on Great Temple, *Antiguedades Mexicanas*, Lienzo de Tlaxcalla, plate 16, published Mexico 1892. Negative #330879. Courtesy Department of Library Services, American Museum of Natural History.

Sir James Frazer (1854-1941). Reprinted by permission of Pitt Rivers Museum, University of Oxford, England.

Culture Areas of North America. Harold E. Driver, *Indians of North America*, The University of Chicago Press.© 1961 The University of Chicago. Reprinted by permission of the publisher.

Grave Creek Burial Mound, West Virginia. Ephraim G. Squier and E.H. Davis, *Ancient Monuments of the Mississippi Valley*, Smithsonian Contributions to Knowledge, vol. I, Washington, D.C., 1848.

Carolus Linnaeus' Biological Classification of Humanity. In *Systema Naturae (1735)*. Courtesy Department of Library Services, American Museum of Natural History.

Comparison of Ape and Human Skeletons. Thomas H. Huxley, *Man's Place in Nature*. The University of Michigan Press © 1959 The University of Michigan. Reprinted by permission of the publisher.

Charles Darwin's Study at Down House, Kent, England. American Philosophical Society, Philadelphia. Darwin's Study at Down House, etching by Haig. Negative #32684.

Courtesy Department of Library Services, American Museum of Natural History.

Chapter 2

Ruth Benedict (1887-1948). Stamp Design © 1995 U.S. Postal Service. Reproduced with permission. All rights reserved.

Alorese Youth Drawings. Cora Du Bois, *The People of Alor*, vol. II, The University of Minnesota Press. Copyright 1944 The University of Minnesota. Reprinted by permission of the publisher.

"The Totemic Operator." Claude Lévi-Strauss, *The Savage Mind*, The University of Chicago Press. © 1962 by Librarie Plon, 8 rue Grancière, Paris-6ᵉ. English trans. © 1966 George Weidenfield and Nicolson Ltd. Reprinted by permission of The University of Chicago Press.

Nuer Seasonality. E.E. Evans-Pritchard, *The Nuer: A Description of the Modes of Livelihood and Political Institutions of a Nilotic People*, 1940, by permission of Oxford University Press.

The Kula Ring. Map from *Cultural Anthropology: A Contemporary Perspective*, by Roger M. Keesing. Copyright © 1976 Holt, Rinehart and Winston. Reproduced by permission of the publisher.

Chapter 3

The Sapir-Whorf Hypothesis. John B. Carroll, ed., *Language, Thought and Reality: Selected Writings of Benjamin Lee Whorf*, M.I.T. Press. Copyright © by The Massachusetts Institute of Technology. Reprinted by permission of the publisher.

Formal Gardens at Castle Bromwich Hall, West Midlands, England. Martin Locock, ed., *Meaningful Architecture: Social Interpretations of Buildings*, Ashgate Publishing. © 1994 Authors.

The publisher has made every effort to locate all copyright holders of the illustrations published in this text and would be pleased to hear from any party not duly acknowledged.

index

Page numbers that refer to illustrations are italicized.

organic solidarity, 92, 93
organismic analogy, 99, 101, 108,
  131, 137, 143
The Origin of Civilization, 50
The Origin of Races, 125
Origin of Species, 45, 64, 66, 67, *68, 72*
*Origin of the Family, Private Property,
  and the State*, 49
original sin, 24
Orphism, 20
orthogenesis, 65
Osiris, 20
*Outline of the Intellectual Progress of
  Mankind*, 36
Oxford University, 50

Pacific Ocean, 26, 65, 66, 80, 82, 87
paleoanthropology, 13
paleontology, 62-63
Paleolithic, 58
paradigms, 140-141
Parker, Ely, 47
participant-observation, 104, 122
patrilateral cross-cousin marriage,
  97
patrilineal descent, 48, 49, 90
patrilocality, 90
Patristic period, 20
Patterns of Culture, 82-83
The People of Alor, 89
personality variables, 90
Perry, William, 53, 55
Persian Empire, 19
phenomenology, 130
phenotype, 127
Philadelphia, 79
philosophical anarchist, 140
phonemes, 95
phonemics, 112
phonetics, 112
phylogeny, 71, 126
physical (biological) anthropology,

  13, 69, 74, 124-129, 147, 148
physics, 73, 76
pietism, 37
Pike, Kenneth, 112-113
*Plans for Two Discourses on Universal
  History*, 36
Plato, 18, 19, 20, 22, 63, 64
Playfair, John, 61
pleasure principle, 85
Poland, 32, 104
Polanyi, Karl, 99
political economy, 109, 135-140
Political Systems of Highland Burma,
  103
Polo, Marco, 26
polyandry, 49
polygenesis, 29, 75
polygenic heredity, 127, 128
polygyny, 90
polytheism, 51
Portugal, 26
positivism, 37-39, 44, 121, 144
Positivism, 38-39
postmodernism, 30, 109, 121, 134,
  135, 140-146, 148-149
post-partum prohibitions, 90
post-processual archaeology, 121,
  134
poststructural, 138, 148
potlatch, 118
practice, 143
Prague School, 95
The Praise of Folly, 24
praxis, 143
Pre-Historic Times, 58
prehistory, 41, 44, 56-59, 120-121
pre-Socratics, 17
primal patricide, 86
primary cultural institutions, 88-89
primatology, 13, 124, 125, 129
The Primeval Antiquities of Denmark,
  56